Flying V
Explorer
Firebird

Flying V
Explorer
Firebird

Dave Mustaine of Megadeth at Download 2010 with his Flying V-influenced Dean VMNT signature model

AN ODD-SHAPED HISTORY OF GIBSON'S WEIRD ELECTRIC GUITARS **TONY BACON**

FLYING V, EXPLORER, FIREBIRD
AN ODD-SHAPED HISTORY OF GIBSON'S WEIRD ELECTRIC GUITARS
TONY BACON

A BACKBEAT BOOK
First edition 2011
Published by Backbeat Books
An Imprint of Hal Leonard Corporation
7777 West Bluemound Road,
Milwaukee, WI 53213
www.backbeatbooks.com

Devised and produced for Backbeat Books by
Outline Press Ltd
2A Union Court, 20-22 Union Road,
London SW4 6JP, England
www.jawbonepress.com

ISBN: 978-i-61713-008-3

A catalogue record for this book is available from the British Library.

Text copyright © 2011 by Tony Bacon. Volume copyright © 2011 by Outline Press Ltd. All rights reserved. No part of this book may be reproduced in any form without written permission, except by a reviewer quoting brief passages in a review. For more information you must contact the publisher.

DESIGN: Paul Cooper Design
EDITOR: Siobhan Pascoe

Printed by Regent Publishing Services Limited, China

11 12 13 14 15 5 4 3 2 1

Contents

FLYING V, EXPLORER, FIREBIRD

EARLY YEARS	**8**
THE FIFTIES	**12**
THE SIXTIES	**36**
THE SEVENTIES	**58**
THE EIGHTIES	**92**
THE NINETIES	**104**
RECENT YEARS	**112**
ENDNOTES	**116**

THE REFERENCE LISTING

HOW TO USE THE LISTINGS	**118**
MODEL LISTINGS	**119**
SERIAL NUMBERS	**133**
MODEL CHRONOLOGY	**135**

| INDEX | **137** |
| ACKNOWLEDGEMENTS | **141** |

> "The swept-back, modernistic lines of these really 'forward-looking' instruments will be a real asset to the combo musician with a flair for showmanship."
>
> GIBSON PROMOTES THE NEW FLYING V AND EXPLORER MODELS, 1958

THE
FLYING V
EXPLORER
FIREBIRD
STORY

California, 1965. The owner of the music store turns the key and opens the door to admit his famous visitor, who has been waiting outside for him to arrive, keen to replace a stolen guitar. Dave Davies of The Kinks moves quickly to the rack of guitars inside. He picks up an SG and plugs it in. He turns up the volume, then turns up his nose. He reaches for a Strat, tries it, and declares it too pretty. "What's that up there?" he says, pointing at a few old brown cases. Some heaving and grunting later, they open a case to reveal something different. Dave pops it on, wrestles a little, hooks his arm through the crook in the guitar's body, and belts out the start of 'All Day And All Of The Night'. He nods to his aide, who starts peeling off $20 notes, stopping as the store guy says 200 is right. Everyone is happy: store guy has sold a guitar he's had hanging around for years; aide can get his charge back for an early soundcheck; and Dave has a real Gibson he's never seen before. The old Flying V is finally set to make its new mark.

When histories of the Gibson company reach 1958, suddenly they go widescreen. In that epoch-making year, Gibson salesmen found they had a long line of spectacular new models to shout about. There were the radical Explorer and Flying V solidbodies, a fresh Sunburst finish for the Les Paul Goldtop, the revolutionary semi-solid ES-335 and 355 models, a new double-cutaway body for the Les Paul Junior and Special, and the company's first double-neck electrics. To a greater or lesser extent, all would become classics over the coming years – and today some of them qualify as the most revered electric guitars ever made.

The most unexpected oddities among Gibson's new models for 1958 were the Explorer and Flying V. It's almost impossible today to imagine how dramatically these guitars confounded the expectations of guitar-makers and guitarists alike. There had always been an unwritten law that the body of a guitar must follow a traditional shape. After these two new models appeared, anything seemed possible. And as we'll discover, they inspired later makers to new levels of invention and creativity. Some musicians, too, would gradually discover their particular charms.

Until Gibson's new Flying V and Explorer of 1958, guitars had familiar rounded outlines to the body, with an upper and lower 'bout' straddling a waisted mid-section. It was this classic symmetrical shape that led to the cliché about a guitar being like a woman's body. This was the shape the instrument had enjoyed for a long time, since its roots in earlier centuries. Every guitar more or less copied the template.

Gibson, too, obediently traced the classic template. Orville H. Gibson, born in 1856 in upstate New York near the Canadian border, began making stringed musical instruments in Kalamazoo, Michigan, by the 1880s. He set himself up properly as a manufacturer of musical instruments in that city around 1895. Orville certainly followed

FLYING V ■ EXPLORER ■ FIREBIRD

the conventional template as far as the body shape of his guitars went, but also he took a refreshingly unconventional approach to the construction of his mandolin-family instruments and oval-soundhole guitars. He hand-carved the tops and backs, and he cut the sides from solid wood, rather than use the conventional method of heating and bending. He was also unusual in not using internal bracing, which he thought degraded volume and tone. Orville understood that the look of his instruments was important, too, and would often have the bodies decorated with beautiful inlaid pickguards and a distinctive crescent-and-star logo on the headstock.

In 1902, a group of businessmen joined him to form the Gibson Mandolin-Guitar Manufacturing company, and the new firm's products were typical of the kinds of fretted stringed instruments produced in the early decades of the 20th century. The mandolin was the most popular, and Gibson would soon find itself among the most celebrated of mandolin makers, thanks largely to its influential F-5 model, introduced in 1922.

Orville left the Gibson company in 1903. He received a regular royalty for the following five years and then a monthly income until his death in 1918. A year earlier, the firm had moved to new premises on Parsons Street, Kalamazoo, which it occupied until 1984. Once Orville left Gibson, the new managers and workers gradually changed his original methods of construction, not only to make production more efficient but also to improve the instruments. Orville's sawed solid-wood sides were replaced with conventional heated-and-bent parts, and his inlaid, integral pickguard was replaced with a unit elevated from the body, devised by Gibson man Lewis Williams (and the type still in use today by many makers of archtop guitars).

More people began to take up the guitar during the late 20s and 30s, and makers worked hard to gain attention by showing themselves to be inventive and forward-thinking. Gibson obliged with more innovations, including Ted McHugh's adjustable truss-rod, designed for neck strengthening – and something else more or less obligatory, still, on today's guitars.

Thanks to the creativity of other gifted employees such as Lloyd Loar, Gibson established individual landmarks, including Loar's L-5 guitar of the early 20s. This, too, had the conventional waisted body shape but with the added novelty of a pair of f-shaped soundholes, known as f-holes, in the top. The L-5 defined the look and sound of the early archtop acoustic guitar. Musicians took to the model and its siblings and used them in a variety of musical styles, none more appealing than the so-called parlour jazz epitomised by the work of Eddie Lang.

As players demanded more volume from their guitars, Gibson dutifully increased sizes but retained the classic outline of its acoustic instruments, introducing the big archtop Super 400 model in 1934 and, later in the decade, the 'jumbo' J-series flat-tops. It was around this time that Gibson sold its first electric guitars, the Electric Hawaiian E-150 cast-aluminium steel guitar in 1935 and, the following year, the EH-150 steel and an f-hole hollowbody, the ES-150 – Gibson's first electric archtop. This marked the start of the company's long-running ES series (the letters meant Electric Spanish).

Gibson stopped guitar production when America entered World War II in 1942. When instrument manufacturing began gradually to recover afterward, the firm's managers concluded that the electric guitar was set to become an important part of its reactivated business. The Chicago Musical Instrument Company (CMI) had bought a controlling interest in Gibson in 1944. Manufacturing remained at the original factory in Kalamazoo, more or less halfway between Chicago and Detroit, while Chicago was the location for Gibson's new sales and administration headquarters at the CMI offices.

Gibson began to alter the traditional body for the first time, developing a series of pioneering models with a body cutaway, breaking the timeless outline. Imaginative guitarists openly welcomed the artistic potential of the cutaway and began to investigate the dusty end of the fingerboard. Significant new electric archtops appeared, including the ES-175 in 1949, Gibson's first electric with a pointed cutaway and a pressed, laminated top. The 175 made a particular impact with electric guitarists in jazz, including Jim Hall and Joe Pass, and, later, Pat Metheny.

In 1951, Gibson launched the Super 400CES and the L-5CES, its most serious cutaway-body electric guitars yet. At first, each came with a pair of Gibson's standard single-coil P-90 pickups, but in 1954 they were changed to the company's more powerful Alnico pickups. The Super 400 has attracted bluesman Robben Ford, country players such as Hank Thompson and Merle Travis, rock'n'roller Scotty Moore, and jazzmen including George Benson and Kenny Burrell. The L-5, too, had its fans over the years, including the jazz guitarist Wes Montgomery and country-jazzer Hank Garland.

Ted McCarty joined Gibson in March 1948 after leaving Wurlitzer, the instrument company and music-store chain, where he'd been since 1936 and trained as a manager. McCarty had been expecting to start a new job as assistant treasurer for a candy company, Brach, but a new offer came in from Maurice Berlin at CMI. Berlin recognised McCarty's qualities as an experienced, capable music-business executive and appointed him as Gibson's general manager. Two years later, in 1950, Berlin promoted the 40-year-old McCarty to the top spot and made him president at Gibson.

Gibson was finding it hard in the post-war years to return to full-scale guitar production, and one of McCarty's early managerial tasks was to get the factory back to efficient working, improving communication within the firm and refining the production systems. "They had foremen in this department and that department, but then I'd come across one that didn't have anybody in charge," said McCarty. "You can't run a factory like that. So I chose a man, John Huis, who had been with Gibson a great many years. He was a foreman at that time, in the finishing department, and I made him superintendent, and he and I worked together. We decided that every day we would go through the factory and find one operation that we thought could be improved."[1]

Managers at all the big guitar manufacturers in the USA, including Gibson, would routinely assess the new models that their rivals introduced. This was usually no more sophisticated a task than wandering over to a booth at one of the regular trade-show gatherings to casually spy on an opponent, or checking out the ads and news announcements of competing firms in the trade press. But as the new decade dawned, some unexpected events meant that more specific action was necessary.

For many in the instruments business, the first sign of something distinctly new in electric guitars came with the 1950 edition of *The Purchaser's Guide To The Music Industries*, an annual US listings book published by *The Music Trades* magazine. An ad inside by the California-based Fender Fine Electric Instruments revealed a ripple of individuality from a company that so far had made little impression. Among the expected steel guitars and small amplifiers was a rather thin-looking cutaway electric guitar of otherwise regular shape – although the headstock, with all six tuners on one side, looked rather different. "Esquire" was the tagline next to the picture of the instrument, and then some further text: "The newest thing in Spanish guitars – fine action, new tone, perfect intonation." What Fender didn't say turned out to be a fundamental point: this was a solidbody electric guitar. It was the first of its kind to be sold commercially, and it would change guitars, guitar-playing, and music. But not immediately.

In the years that followed, Fender gradually built on that first solidbody electric, changing the model's name to Telecaster and adding alongside a solid electric bass, the Precision. Gibson, like its rivals, had its ear to the ground and could not let this new idea slip by unchallenged. Without too much delay, McCarty set a team to work on a Gibson solidbody, and it took them about a year to develop satisfactory prototypes. McCarty concluded that Les Paul – at the time the most famous guitar player in America after recent hits such as 'How High The Moon' – would be the best man to endorse the company's new electric guitar.

Gibson launched its solidbody Les Paul Model, known today as the Goldtop, in 1952. If the materials Gibson used for the body were new – a solid mahogany base with a carved maple cap on top – then the general outline remained firmly traditional, following the established waisted-and-cutaway shape used by more or less every maker.

The original Goldtop sold well at first in relation to Gibson's other models. Electric guitars were catching on and the solidbody style took off, providing Gibson with some good guitars to challenge Fender's ever-increasing sales.

In 1954, Gibson historian Julius Bellson consulted sales records to chart the progress of the company's electric instruments. As a result of his research, he estimated that back in 1938, electric guitars made up no more than ten percent of Gibson guitar sales, but he saw that the proportion of electrics to the rest had risen to 15 percent by 1940, to 50 percent by 1951, and that by 1953, no less than 65 percent of the company's total guitar sales were of electrics.

In a move designed to widen the market still further for its solidbody electric guitars, Gibson issued two more Les Paul models in 1954, the cheaper Junior and the fancier Custom, and a year later added the Les Paul TV model, essentially a Junior in what Gibson referred to as a 'limed mahogany' finish, and also the Special, a two-pickup Junior. A number of well-known guitarists played Gibson Les Pauls in the 50s, including rock'n'roller Frannie Beecher, bluesmen like Guitar Slim, Freddie King, and John Lee Hooker, and rockabilly rebel Carl Perkins. Since then, of course, the Les Paul in its various guises has become a world-beater.

Back in the 50s, Gibson must have been delighted by the success of the new solidbody style, but that didn't mean the company neglected the hollowbody electrics. During 1955, Gibson launched three new models – the ES-225T, ES-350T, and Byrdland – in a new slimmer-body 'thinline' style that aimed at a sort of hybrid of solidbody leanness and hollowbody tradition, intended to be more comfortable than the existing deep-body archtop cutaway electrics. An important player who grasped the possibilities of these friendlier new Gibson electrics was Chuck Berry, the most influential rock'n'roll guitarist of the 50s. Berry chose a brand new natural-finish ES-350T to fuel his startling hybrid of boogie, country, and blues.

It was around this time that Seth Lover developed humbucking pickups in the Gibson workshops. Lover was a radio and electronics expert and had worked for Gibson in the 40s and early 50s, in between jobs for the US Navy. He joined Gibson permanently in 1952, and in the electronics department, run by Walt Fuller, the industrious Lover first developed the Alnico pickup. But he soon set to work on a more important design.

Lover was charged with finding a way to cut down the hum and electrical interference that plagued standard single-coil pickups, including Gibson's ubiquitous P-90, which Fuller had designed. Lover contemplated the humbucking 'choke coil' found in some Gibson amplifiers, installed to eliminate any hum caused by the power transformers. "I thought," recalled Lover, "that if we can make humbucking chokes, then why can't we make humbucking pickups?"[2] No reason at all, he concluded, and started to build prototypes.

The humbucking name comes simply from the way such devices 'buck' or cut hum. The design principle, too, is reasonably simple. A humbucking pickup employs two coils with opposite magnetic polarity, wired together so that they are electrically out-of-phase. The result is a pickup that is less prone to picking up extraneous noise, and one that in the process gives a wonderful clear tone.

Gibson began to use the new humbuckers in the early months of 1957 and started to replace the P-90 single-coil pickups on the Les Paul Goldtop and Custom during that year. The Custom was promoted from two P-90s to three humbuckers, and the new pickups would be used for both the Flying V and the Explorer when they appeared shortly thereafter. Players gradually came to appreciate that humbuckers provided a marvellous tone, and today many guitarists and collectors covet in particular the earliest type, known as a PAF because it had a small label bearing the words "Patent Applied For" attached to the underside.

Lover was not the first to come up with the idea of humbucking pickups, as he discovered when he came to patent the design (as assignor to Gibson). The patent attorneys made reference to no fewer than six previous efforts. The earliest, dating from 1935, was Armand F. Knoblaugh's patent for Baldwin, apparently made with an electric piano in mind but specifically offered as appropriate to other steel-string instruments. "I had a hell of a time getting a patent," Lover remembered, "and I finally got one with more or less one claim: that I'd built a humbucking pickup."[3] Ray Butts came up with a similar principle around the same time while working with Gretsch, for whom he designed the Filter'Tron humbucking pickup.

Lover and Gibson applied for their patent in June 1955, and it was eventually issued in July 1959 – which explains that PAF label. Or does it? The PAF labels appeared on pickups on guitars dated up to 1962 – well after the patent was issued. Lover explained this. "Gibson didn't want to give any information as to what patent to look up for those who wanted to make copies. I think that was the reason they carried on with the PAF label for quite a while."[4] When Gibson did eventually get around to putting a patent number on the pickup, the company again deterred budding copyists by 'mistakenly' using the number for Les Paul's trapeze bridge-and-tailpiece patent.

Some players say they prefer the sound of original PAF-label humbuckers (and the subsequent 'patent-number' pickups). They consider later humbuckers to have a poorer tone, apparently caused by small changes to coil-winding, magnet grades, and wire-sheathing. Lover could not recall any alterations made to his invention during the transition from those that had the PAF label to the later units stamped with patent numbers. "The only change that I'm aware of," he said, "is that from time to time Gibson would use gold plating on the covers. And I think if the gold plating got a little heavy, then the pickups would tend to lose the high frequencies – because gold is a very good conductor."[5]

Meanwhile, the growing success of the Fender operation was not lost on Gibson's managers. Some of them probably thought that Gibson was stuck in a Midwest frame of mind and in danger of falling behind the times. Over on the West Coast, Fender continued to turn out solidbody electric guitars that looked bright and modern, especially the new Stratocaster model that had been doing so well since its launch in 1954. More and more musicians and budding musicians were buying Fender's solidbody electrics.

The Stratocaster was a stunner. It seemed in some ways to owe more to contemporary automobile design than traditional guitar forms, especially in the flowing curves of its beautifully proportioned body. It defiantly moved away from the classic symmetrical guitar template, bravely throwing the shape forward with offset, opposed cutaways. It was the embodiment of tailfin-flash 50s American design. Even the shape of the pickguard complemented the body lines perfectly, and the overall impression was of a guitar where all the components suited one another with style and verve. It seemed excitingly new and it had a modern space-age name. Gibson had to compete.

One of the most important parts of Ted McCarty's job was to keep the massive Gibson operation at full capacity. In the late 50s, Gibson had around 350 people on the payroll at Kalamazoo. That's a lot of mouths to feed, and McCarty had to ensure they were kept busy. The sales people out in the field relayed the chatter that Gibson was beginning to seem old-fashioned and – aside from the Les Paul models and Chuck's 350 – to look as if they made electric guitars mostly for the old-school jazz players rather than the new (and potentially lucrative) rock'n'rollers.

"Leo Fender was always downgrading us," McCarty recalled later, adding with a hollow laugh: "Which is why I was so fond of him. He was going around the country saying that Gibson was a stodgy old company, that we'd never had a new idea in our lives, that we were still making things like we did 50 years ago. He was saying that our line was all stodgy things and his was the bright new deal."[6]

McCarty decided to play Fender at its own modern-design game. Soon – probably in the spring of 1957 – his team came up with a plan to produce three new 'Modernistic' models that would dispose of Gibson's fusty old conventional guitar shapes and introduce instead some shockingly new of-the-moment designs. "We were getting ready to think about the summer trade show," said McCarty, "and we were thinking: 'What can we come up with that's new or different?' I said, you know what? Let's make some guitars that are so outlandish, they'll cause a stir at the show. We'll prove to Leo that we can make something different."[7] The three proposed models would become known as the Flying V, the Explorer, and the Moderne.

It's not clear exactly how many people at the company were involved in the design team for the new instruments. Years later, when I asked McCarty about those responsible for guitar design at Gibson in the 50s, he told me there were at least four, including himself. A good deal of McCarty's job was to inspire and lead, and he seems to have been brilliant at doing just that. And presumably, like any good manager, he knew the value of delegation. It's possible he may have overstated in later interviews his own practical involvement in the design process back in the classic Gibson years. He had a big company to run, and he wouldn't necessarily have been involved in the detailed daily action and decision-making.

McCarty said the 50s design team consisted of John Huis, who was his number two and in charge of production, plus "one of the fellows in charge of the wood department", which may be a reference to the company's chief woodworking engineer at the time, Larry Allers, and also "one of the guitar players in final assembly", by which he was probably referring to Rem Wall.[8]

Gil Hembree, who researched deeply into the story of Gibson employees for his 2007 book *Gibson Guitars: Ted McCarty's Golden Era*, considers Allers an unsung hero. "In 1957 and '58, Larry was in charge of the 'whitewood' shop, the pattern-makers, and the machine shop," Hembree says. "He was the one who would have organised the work on the Modernistic guitars, selecting one of the pattern-makers and giving them the assignment. It's certainly possible that he might have tweaked some of this prototype work on them, because he had fine skills. Not only did Larry supervise, explain, and coordinate, but also he would have done some of the most difficult hand work on the designs."[9]

McCarty named two further Gibson men who were usually part of the design think-tank in the 50s: Julius Bellson, who was assistant treasurer and personnel manager, and Wilbur Marker, service and custom-instruments manager. Also, McCarty said, it was natural and essential to consult Gibson's sales team as part of new-model development, which he did through Clarence Havenga, vice president in charge of sales. Havenga was apparently known throughout the Gibson building as Mister Guitar. In the company's promotional magazine, the *Gibson Gazette*, the official line emphasised that work on the designs for the Modernistic trio and the other new models of the late 50s was done by a team, which it described as "a task force of engineers and craftsmen".[10]

When I spoke some time later to Seth Lover, inventor of Gibson's humbucking pickup, he told me that he'd been significantly involved in the Modernistic guitars. Lover pointed out a Flying V in an old Gibson catalogue and asked if I remembered it. "That's a body style I designed for them when I was at Gibson," he said proudly. "The idea behind that was to get some new shapes, and I designed this. I sketched out a number of shapes and styles that I thought would be different for guitars, rather than going back to older designs."[11]

The first evidence of the search for new and refreshed approaches came in June 1957, when Gibson filed three patent applications for the new designs. (Two were filed on June 20 1957, while the third, for the Flying V, was filed a week later, on June 27. The US Patent Office eventually issued the three resulting design patents on January 7 1958.) Each gave the name of Gibson president Ted McCarty as 'assignor', which was normal practice. It didn't mean these were solely McCarty's designs, but derived from the legal procedure that required one individual's name to be on a patent. McCarty, as head of the firm, was the natural candidate. The legal point of a patent is to grant the inventor the right to prevent others from making and selling the same item.

The Patent Office issues two broad types of patent: the first kind is intended for an original 'ornamental design'; the other for a 'new and useful' invention. Design patents tend to be simple depictions of the object in question, while patents for inventions are often necessarily more complex documents. The three Gibson design patents were indeed simple. Each single-sheet document was a claim for the "ornamental design for a stringed musical instrument, as shown and described" and was illustrated with two modest line-drawings next to one another: "a top plan view of a stringed musical instrument showing my new design" and "a side elevation view thereof".

It was unusual for Gibson to apply for this simple type of design patent: most often, the company applied for invention patents, which had detailed mechanical plans and full descriptions of the finished item. For example, the invention patent for the Tune-o-matic bridge, issued in April 1956, had a page of meticulous drawings with 35 keyed parts, plus more than 2,000 words of descriptions and claims.

What prompted Gibson's sudden interest in design patents? It seems that with these three stark Modernistic-guitar patents, Gibson was again playing Leo Fender at his own game. Fender had claimed simple 'ornamental design' patents for the Telecaster and the Precision Bass, issued in 1951 and 1952 respectively. McCarty told me that he patented the three new Gibson designs, for the guitars that became known as the Moderne, Flying V, and Explorer, because he "knew what Leo would do" – presumably meaning he expected that something like a Fender Flying V-type model might follow. "If I had a patent, however, he wouldn't dare," said McCarty. "I never bothered with patenting a lot of the other models, because it costs money to patent a guitar shape."[12]

As usual with new patents, attorneys made a search for any similar prior claims, and for the three new Gibson designs they came up with five previous "references cited". The earliest two were from 1887 and 1916, each for a fanciful violin with a triangular-shaped body, while a further one from 1949 looked as if the sides of a regular violin had been squared-off. There was also a slant-sided ukulele design from a couple of years later. But the attorneys found no earlier guitar patents with similar non-standard designs during their doubtless thorough search.

The first Gibson patent, numbered 181,865, was for what we now recognise as an early attempt at the design that became the Explorer. This precise version would itself become known as the Futura. It had an angular body shape, very similar to what ended up as the Explorer but with a narrower waist, and a 'split' headstock in the shape of an offset V. The regular drooping Explorer headstock evidently came a little later in the design process. The bare-bones line drawing showed two humbucking pickups and a Tune-o-matic bridge plus tailpiece, but there were no controls, no pickguard, and no fingerboard markers.

The second patent, 181,866, was for the design that became known as the Moderne and, to many vintage-guitar fans, as the one that got away – of which more later. The patent illustrated an unattractive design with a body that looked something like the top half of a Flying V combined with a stubby curved base. It was as if someone had wanted a Flying V that might be comfortable to play sitting down ... but had completely disregarded the aesthetics. The headstock appeared as if a regular Gibson head had been squashed and smeared off, resulting in another ugly shape. Like the Explorer patent, this drawing featured pickups and a bridge and tailpiece, but it too lacked controls, pickguard, and fingerboard markers. As we'll discover, there is strong evidence that this particular design went no further than the patent, at least for now. It's hard to conclude that Gibson made anything but the correct decision.

The third patent in this group of three new 'ornamental designs', number 181,867, was for the instrument that became the Flying V. Like the other two, the rough drawing of the guitar's front and side lacked some features but had others – and one item that was definitely present was the distinctive V-shaped tailpiece, clearly an idea that came along relatively early in the process and that would stay with the design.

With the patent applications in, the next major step for Gibson's new approach to guitar design came at the 1957 NAMM show. Instrument companies officially unveiled new instruments during this trade-only convention, staged annually by the National Association of Music Merchants. All the leading instrument-business people would attend, from store managers to manufacturers, making it the most important trade gathering of the year. In '57, the show was at the Palmer House hotel in Chicago from Monday July 15 to Thursday 18, with Gibson exhibiting under the banner of its parent company, Chicago Musical Instrument, in rooms 726–729. "We always had displays at trade shows," said McCarty. "The different companies would rent a suite or a room in places like the Palmer House, and visitors would go around from room to room to see what was new and available."[13]

Gibson caused a stir at the '57 NAMM show when they showed at least one prototype of a Modernistic guitar. It was a rough mock-up of a Futura, the name that has since been applied to the early version of the model that became the Explorer. *Piano Trade Magazine* provided the sole evidence, printing a small photograph in a review of the show in its September issue. Gibson's sales manager Clarence Havenga is pictured laughing and clutching a prototype guitar as he stands next to a visitor from the Lyon & Healy chain of stores. The caption offers no information beyond the identity of the two men. Havenga holds a guitar that looks very much like a dummy based on the Futura/Explorer patent drawing: it has pickups, a bridge, and a tailpiece, but no controls; the body wood, possibly korina, looks unfinished; the neck has a complete rosewood fingerboard (and unlike the patent it does have markers); and the head is in the shape of a V.

It's a frustrating photo in some ways. The only other guitar visible in the frame is one of the new double-neck guitars, also presumably in prototype form (production of that model would not start until the following year). What we certainly do not see is any evidence at all of the other two patented Modernistic guitar designs. We'll probably never know for sure if Gibson also had a prototype of the Flying V and the Moderne at the '57 NAMM show.

My guess is that a Flying V was there, in some form. McCarty said that Gibson made sales decisions based on feedback from the trade shows. "We would take prototypes to the show, show them, and they'd get a reaction from the dealers," he explained. "According to the reaction, we'd go back to the factory, and the salesmen would say: 'This one is a good seller; that one is a good seller; but I couldn't do much with this one.' That's how we chose the line, you might say."[14] There must surely have been a Flying V at the show as well as a Futura/Explorer, simply because we know that Gibson later made the decision to put those two into production. It seems less likely that a sample of the Moderne was there, and it may be that Gibson had already decided it was the least impressive of the three and never went further with it than the design patent.

One intriguing guitar that may illuminate this part of the story is an early version of the Flying V made by Gibson to help one of its case manufacturers, Geib of Chicago, produce a custom case for the production model. This early V turned up in the 90s and was sold then as a desirable collectable. It differs from the production model in that it has a black pickguard and a gold-coloured logo. The control pots date to 1957, and it's tempting to speculate that this prototype could have been displayed at the '57 NAMM show in Chicago and then given to Geib. But speculation is all it can be.

Beyond the patent applications and the trade-show sighting, another early public sign of Gibson's refreshed attitude to guitar design came in a New Products Issue of the *Gibson Gazette* dated November 1957. "Do you believe in magic? Probably not," the article began. "We take a skeptical view of it, too. But Gibson engineers and craftsmen have come up with a line of products that amounts to sheer magic to us." The *Gazette* explained that Gibson had showed a "fine group of new instruments and amplifiers" at the recent NAMM show but now wanted to present these "milestone" products in the magazine so that dealers and musicians who hadn't made it to Chicago could see the startling new stuff for themselves.

The Flying V was the sole guitar from the Modernistic trio previewed in the November *Gazette*, implying that Gibson had by now evaluated the feedback from NAMM and singled out the V as the Modernistic instrument most likely to appeal to dealers and guitarists. Under a picture of the model, the article continued excitedly: "Russia has her satellite, perhaps to the embarrassment of the US, but the Gibson folks have come forth with their own 'first' – the futuristic Flying V guitar. The swept-back, tapered lines of this really forward-looking instrument will be a real asset to the combo musician with a flair for showmanship." It was a prescient comment, coming from a world where the flamboyant metal guitarist – unquestionably a musician with a "flair for showmanship" – was still many years away from birth and adolescence.

The picture of the Flying V in the *Gazette* looked suspiciously as if it was at least partly hand-done, perhaps a pen-and-wash illustration. Putting aside the question of whether it was entirely real, there are a number of differences compared to the later production version. It had a dark finish, which some have assumed meant that, if this sample was real, it was made from mahogany rather than korina; it had an open rout on the lower body edge where the ridged-rubber strip would later go; there was a long neck heel that reached to the 14th fret; the pickguard did not continue between the pickups; what looked like an output jack sat on the inside of the lower body 'leg' rather than on the face of that leg; there was no pickup selector; and the raised Gibson logo was on an extended truss-rod cover.

The *Gazette* added: "The swept-back design permits complete accessibility of the full guitar register … the 22-fret rosewood fingerboard has *all* frets clear of the body. The modernistic pickguard and tailpiece are of matching design." This marked the first appearance of the word 'modernistic' in relation to a Gibson guitar. As a final note, there was some information about the look of the Flying V, which would be offered in "natural limed Korina finish".[15] This harked back to the limed finish that Gibson had used earlier in the decade on the mahogany bodies of Les Paul TVs and Specials. The *Gazette* feature prompted one musical-instruments trade magazine to comment briefly on the new Gibson guitar in its December 1957 issue, with a journalist noting that the Flying V guitar was a "striking Gibson innovation" designed "in the shape of a V" and made in "the finest quality Korina hardwood".[16]

The Flying V was given its name by Seth Lover, the Gibson electronics engineer who, as we've seen, had designed its humbucking pickups and may even have been responsible for the model's overall look. "When Seth saw the first one he laughed and said, well, that looks like a flying v," McCarty recalled later. "So we named it the Flying V."[17]

At the Gibson factory in Kalamazoo, production of the Flying V was about to start. February 21 1958 turned out to be an important day at the plant. Managers would log production in a ledger, the so-called day book, filling in by hand the instruments produced each day. That Friday, among the instruments logged were five remarkable guitars, noted specially as "Memo Display CMI", presumably referring to an official memo from Gibson's parent company, Chicago Musical Instruments, requesting these guitars. 'Display' was the general Gibson term for shows and exhibitions – Ward Arbanas had the job of supervisor of displays – but there was no important show taking place around this time, so the instruction is something of a mystery. Perhaps it meant these guitars would be displayed for authorisation to pass them to full production? The list itself was less mysterious: it included entries for the first examples of "Dbl neck Mandolin", "ES-335T", "EB-2", and "LP Cherry Red", but at the top was an entry for "Flying V in Korena". It marked a significant moment for one of the most radical electric guitars that Gibson or anyone else had ever made.

A month or so later, Gibson issued a new illustrated catalogue for its electric guitar line, superseding the previous one dated October 1957. A striking half-page splash on the back featured the Flying V for the first time, using the same pen-and-wash illustration that had appeared in the *Gazette* a few months earlier. "Gibson leads the way with this 'design of the future'," began the triumphant blurb, continuing with further lines that were familiar from the earlier promo efforts, but now with the m-word in place. "The swept-back, modernistic lines of this really 'forward-looking' instrument will be a real asset to the combo musician with a flair for showmanship." The catalogue copy finished with a note on the pickups. "The new humbucking pickup generates more power and creates greater clarity and sustaining tone while reducing hum from outside interference."

The price of the Flying V in that catalogue, dated March 1958, was $247.50 (the equivalent of about $1,900 in today's money). A special 'plush case' was available for $75. (These were zone 1 prices; for zone 2, they were $262.50 for the V and $77.50 for the case. The two zones reflected Gibson's higher shipping costs to the furthest US states, west of the Rocky Mountains, which were grouped in zone 2.) The price for the Flying V in 1958 was exactly the same as that for the Les Paul Goldtop, putting it more or less half way up the pricelist of Gibson's electric guitars: the $700 Natural-finish Super 400-CES sat at the top, with the $120 Sunburst-finish Les Paul Junior at the bottom. Over at Fender, the Stratocaster was pitched a touch higher than the V, at $274.50, while the Telecaster was quite a bit lower, at $199.50.

One early and unusual order for a Flying V was shipped on April 9, marked intriguingly in Gibson records as being without serial number and "(for Alaska) CMI, plush". A few Gibson dealers began to receive stock of the new model toward the end of that month. Recipients of the first batch of four Flying Vs, shipped on Monday 21st, included a Colonial Music store in Ohio and a Lyon & Healy store, probably in Chicago. It seems that the Lyon & Healy visitor at Gibson's NAMM booth the previous summer – the one photographed with the prototype Futura/Explorer – must have placed an order while he was there. A bigger batch of ten Vs was shipped out of the Kalamazoo factory the following week, on the 30th. One V appears to have been shipped twice in May, at first to Gibson's Canadian distributor, Turner Musical Instrument, perhaps on loan for a dealer event, before being returned and reshipped a week or so later to a New York store.

The most obvious visual feature of the production version of the new guitar was, of course, the astonishing V-like body with its angular arrowhead shape. Gibson described it as a "solid body of finest Korina hardwood in natural limed finish". Years later, I asked McCarty if he could recall why Gibson chose korina for the Flying V. "Because it's like a whiter mahogany," he replied. "There was a period of time there in which players wanted Blonde guitars: they had a desire for that light colour. We wanted a Blonde instrument, and so the Flying Vs were Blonde instruments, made of korina. Korina is not really white – it's a little on the yellow side, a sort-of Blonde."

Fender's Telecaster and Esquire had a Blonde finish as standard, and at the 1957 NAMM show Fender had displayed a Stratocaster in Blonde with gold hardware. Gibson may have noticed what a striking combination this made. "We wanted a Blonde instrument, and the nearest thing we could think of was limba, or korina," McCarty concluded. "It was a little lighter than mahogany, but it handled about the same: you could cut it and it didn't splinter as much as a lot of things."[18]

The name korina was a US tradename for the West African hardwood Terminalia superba, usually known as limba, or afara. Limba is sometimes compared to mahogany in terms of its average weight and its tonal characteristics for solidbody guitars, but it's a different species and family. Gibson seems to have chosen it primarily for the attractive look and light colour, which provided a light-finished 'limed' or Blonde-like appearance – but, crucially, without the extra work that mahogany requires to achieve a similar effect. Gibson was already using pale korina for the Skylark lap-steel guitar, launched in 1957, so there was probably some already available at the factory, or at least relatively easily available from an existing supplier. Gibson had also used the wood for its Consolette steel, a model dropped during 1957.

The new Flying V's korina body had two 'legs' making the V shape, and these had gently rounded ends and formed a rounded 'crotch'. There was a very subtle curving of the squared shoulders where the neck joined the body. There was a deep rout cut into the front of the body to take the pickups and controls, and it was covered by the pickguard. A narrow black ridged-rubber strip, cut from floor-mat material, was glued to the lower edge of the body, intended to stop the guitar slipping should the musician choose to play it sitting down.

The Flying V had a one-piece korina neck and followed Gibson's regular assembly method, where the neck would be glued to the body with the aid of a tight mortise-and-tenon joint. Unusually for Gibson, the body wood overlaps the neck heel at the back. There were twenty-two metal frets on a rosewood fingerboard glued to the face of the neck, over a channel in which sat a strengthening metal truss-rod. The rod could be fine-tuned to correct neck misalignment using a special tool to turn an adjustment nut, which was located under a cover on the headstock.

In the face of the fingerboard were small circular pearloid plastic position-markers, known as dot markers because of their shape, inlaid in front of the third, fifth, seventh, ninth, twelfth, fifteenth, seventeenth, nineteenth, and twenty-first frets, with the twelfth-fret octave position marked by a pair of dots. Corresponding to these positions, on the top side of the neck as viewed by the player, were nine smaller white position dots, again with a double-dot marking the twelfth-fret position. At the top of the fingerboard was the nut, of white plastic, which stopped and spaced the strings there. The scale length was twenty-four-and-three-quarter inches, the same as for the existing Les Paul solidbody electrics.

The headstock was a three-piece construction consisting of a centre section with glued-on sides. It was a variant on the traditional Gibson three-tuners-each-side design, with a wide base that tapered in a V shape to a rounded tip, something like the body shape in miniature. Screwed to the rear of the headstock were six individual Kluson

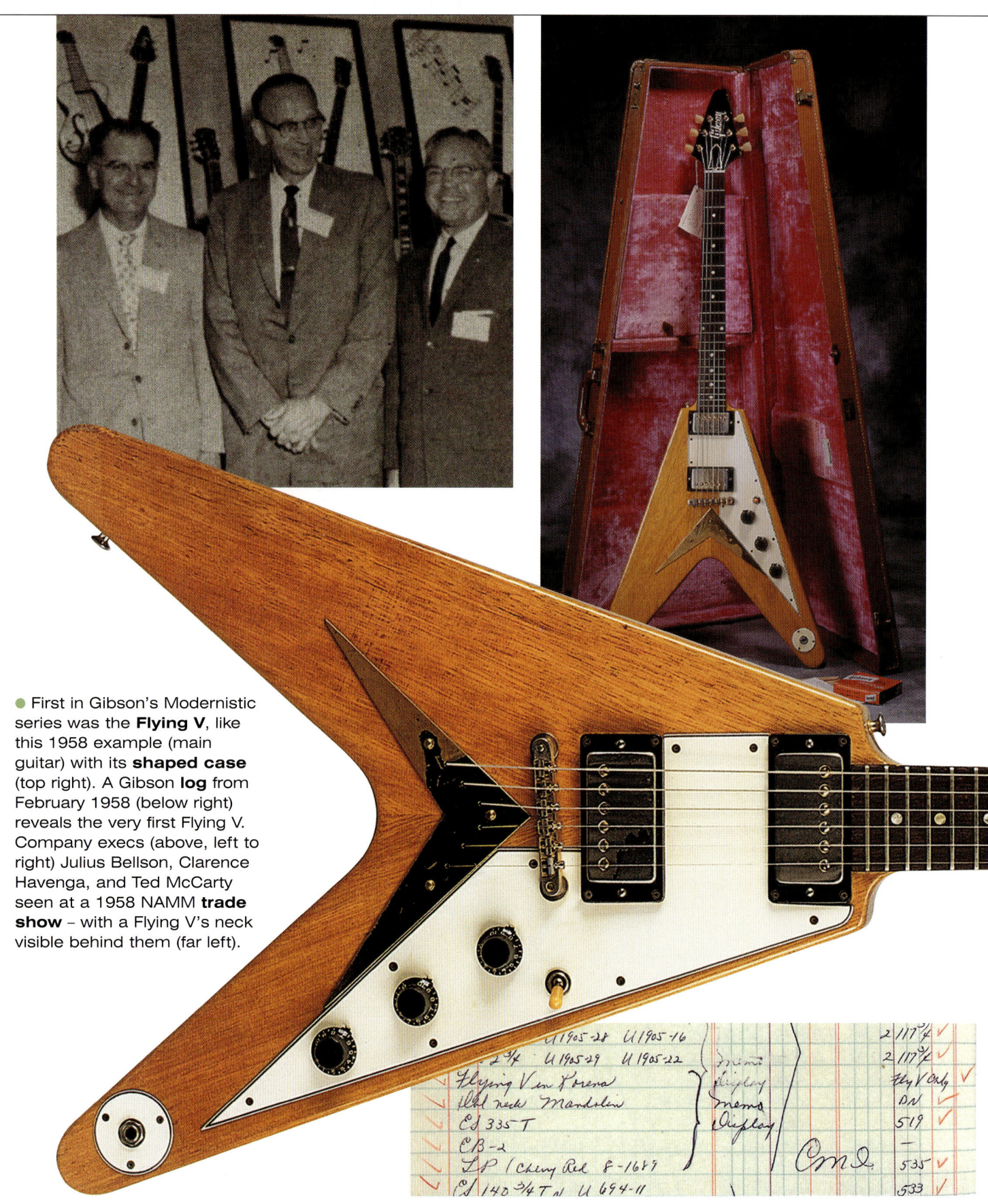

● First in Gibson's Modernistic series was the **Flying V**, like this 1958 example (main guitar) with its **shaped case** (top right). A Gibson **log** from February 1958 (below right) reveals the very first Flying V. Company execs (above, left to right) Julius Bellson, Clarence Havenga, and Ted McCarty seen at a 1958 NAMM **trade show** – with a Flying V's neck visible behind them (far left).

FLYING V ■ EXPLORER ■ FIREBIRD

FLYING V CLEARED FOR TAKE-OFF

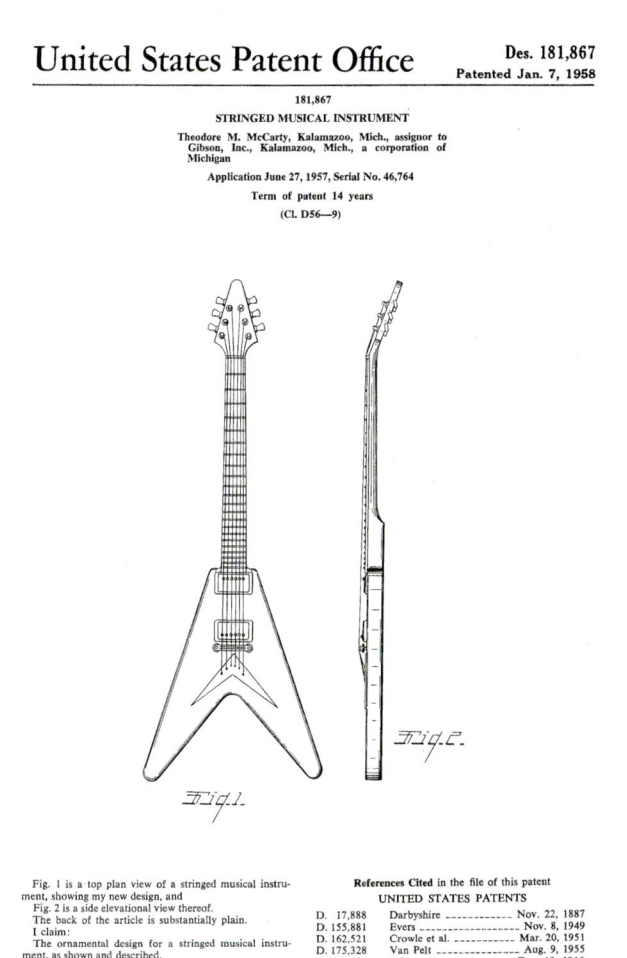

● The first public sign of Gibson's revolutionary new Flying V had come in summer 1957 with the application for a simple **design patent** (above left). The pressure for Gibson to design a modern-looking solidbody guitar came from Fender, whose sleek and attractive Stratocaster model was launched in 1954. This **Fender ad** (above right) was one of several published in the late 50s by the upstart California maker underlining its of-the-moment outlook. Gibson, meanwhile, was seen as more traditional, and its staid ads often featured jazzmen such as **Herb Ellis** (left) who played old-style guitars. With the Flying V, however, Gibson suddenly showed a new-found flair for modern style.

FLYING V ■ EXPLORER ■ FIREBIRD   23

tuners, each with a closed metal back and a plastic acorn-shape plastic button on a thin metal shaft, which passed through the headstock. On the face of the headstock, each string was wound around the tuner's protruding shaft, which had a hole through the top to help secure the string. Between the tuner shafts was a raised silver-coloured plastic Gibson logo, as also used on some of the company's amplifiers, and a traditional bell-shaped plastic truss-rod cover. There was an inked-on serial number on the rear of the headstock, under the clear lacquer, with the first digit – 8 or 9 – indicating the year of production as 1958 or 1959.

Gibson fitted various items to the guitar. There were two metal strap buttons, one screwed to the inside of the upper 'leg' of the body and the other to the top body shoulder. A triple-layer pickguard of white/black/white plastic was fixed to the body with eight screws. The pickguard had almost all the electrical components and wiring fitted to its underside. On the face of the guard were three control knobs and a three-way selector switch. Underneath, and thus hidden from view, was the circuitry: three potentiometers or pots for the single tone and two volume controls; the body of the selector-switch mechanism; and various soldered hook-up wires to connect everything together.

The pair of identical pickups each had two bobbins inside, wound with plain enamelled wire, one with slugs, the other adjustable screws, plus a tiny metal keeper bar underneath, an alnico magnet, and a piece of wood acting as a spacer. Each had a baseplate, a metal cover with the adjustable screws visible through the top, and a black plastic mounting ring that fixed to the body with four screws, plus a screw each side for height adjustment.

Gibson used a different control layout on the V to the one it generally offered on two-humbucker electrics: the player was offered a volume knob per pickup but just one overall tone control. The three black plastic control knobs were arranged in a line on the Flying V's pickguard, each attached to the top of one of the shafts of the three pots. The knobs became known as bonnet, bell, or top-hat types, named for their shape in profile, and each had a small metal pointer-dial fixed underneath. As the guitarist looked down to play his instrument, the knob nearest the bridge was the neck-pickup volume, then bridge-pickup volume, and, furthest from him, the master tone. Each knob was marked with the numerals 0 to 10 around the flared skirt at the base.

Next to the front volume control was a three-way selector switch, which had a metal lever with a white plastic tip. In the 'up' position the switch selected the neck pickup, 'down' the bridge pickup, and in the centre both pickups. The output jack was located separately, beyond the pickguard, on the top face of the body's lower 'leg'. It was housed in a circular three-ply plastic disc, which was fitted to the body with three screws.

There was a gold-plated zinc-alloy Tune-o-matic bridge, Gibson's model ABR-1, with six brass saddles and two plated zinc adjustment wheels. The stylish tailpiece, specially made for the Flying V, was a V-wing-shaped piece of gold-plated brass, known later as the

Cadillac tailpiece because of its similarity to the car-maker's logo, fixed to the body with three brads. The strings passed over the bridge and then through holes in the tailpiece, travelling through the body to terminate at six anchoring ferrules on the rear (in a similar fashion to Fender's Telecaster, Esquire, and recent Stratocaster). All the visible metal parts were gold-plated, with the exception of the frets. The optional case was specially made by Geib to fit the guitar. It was of a long triangular shape with a flattened tip, had Gibson's familiar high-end brown covering, and inside had a red or pink plush lining – a suitably luxurious bed for such a remarkable creation.

Following the introduction of the Flying V, Gibson set about issuing the second of the new Modernistic models, the Explorer. The company sent a letter to its dealers in May 1958, which author André Duchossoir unearthed later. It alerted the dealers to the latest catalogue and drew their attention to several items within. "Just the other day you received the new Gibson Electric catalog," began the letter, dated May 7. "Why don't you get it out and follow along as we point out some of the very latest features in Gibson electric instruments and amplifiers?"

Top of the list of these pointers was an item headed "Modernistic Design". The letter continued with the familiar blurb on the Flying V, but suddenly came some startling news. "Then there's the Explorer, another ultra-modern design. This guitar is so new you won't find it in the catalog, but it is featured in the April–May issue of the *Gibson Gazette* mailed a few days ago."

On page six of that issue of Gibson's promotional magazine, alongside the now-familiar picture of the dark-body Flying V, was the very first public sighting anywhere of the brand new Explorer. The illustration of the latest guitar revealed a light-coloured body and the same pen-and-wash-like appearance of most of Gibson's catalogue pictures at the time. "Gibson looks to the future and finds truly inspirational design ideas," ran the stirring *Gazette* copy.

Under the headline 'The Forward Look' and pictures of the Explorer and V, the blurb continued: "Breathtaking results of such daring are the two, new dynamic instruments pictured here. We introduce you to a new star in the Gibson line, The Explorer, designed as companion instrument to the already famous Flying V." Then came the standard line, yet again: "The impressive appearance of either modernistic guitar would be a real asset to the combo musician with a flair for showmanship. Engineering for both instruments is identical – they are dissimilar in shape only."[19]

The delay to the launch of the Explorer was probably caused by the modifications that Gibson made to the earlier prototype, known today as the Futura, and its name may have been inspired by the launch of America's first Earth satellite, Explorer-I, at the end of January 1958. Fender was not the sole inhabitant of the stratosphere, it seemed. Compared to the earlier patent drawing and at least one prototype, the body of the new Explorer had a slightly wider waist, a set of more refined lines, and a generally more

● Following on from its Flying V, Gibson launched a second Modernistic model later in 1958, the **Explorer**. This, too, was an angular, modern guitar, wth the accent on straight lines where most previous designs had been based on curves. Gibson made some early Explorers with a V-shape '**split headstock**', like the example shown here (main guitar). It was at one time owned by the guitarist **Rick Derringer**, who is pictured with it (left) on-stage in the 70s. Derringer, who played with Steely Dan and Johnny Winter among others, made a number of modifications to the instrument, including an extra switch below the bridge pickup.

FLYING V ■ EXPLORER ■ FIREBIRD

EARLY EXPLORATION

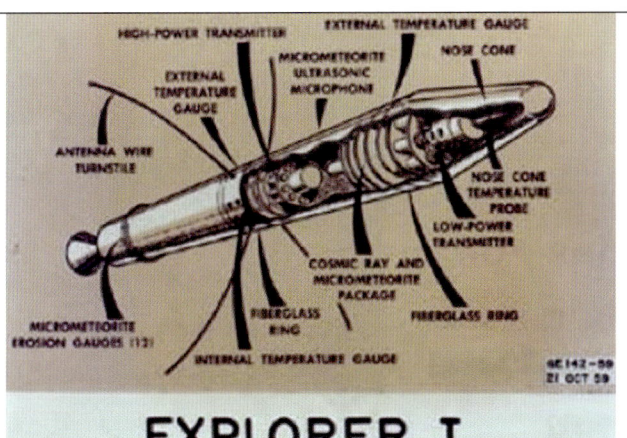
EXPLORER I

● Gibson may have named its new guitar after America's first earth **satellite**, Explorer-I (left), to counter Fender's space-age names like Stratocaster. The **design patent** for the Explorer (bottom left) has differences to the production model, seen also in the crude mock-up which Gibson showed at a 1957 NAMM **trade show** (below right). This early design later became known as the Futura.

FLYING V ■ EXPLORER ■ FIREBIRD

pleasing balance between the constituents. The outcome was the most remarkable guitar design of the 50s, an uncompromising study in offset rectangles.

The evidence points to Explorer production beginning around early July 1958. We'll see in a moment how Gibson's frustratingly incomplete production records indicate this. The April–May *Gazette* pointed that way, too, concluding its piece on the new pair with an estimate that delivery of the Explorer was at least two months away. A new Gibson pricelist, dated July 1 1958, included the new Explorer as well as the existing Flying V under the heading Modernistic Guitars, with both instruments at $247.50.

The 1958 NAMM show was again held at the Palmer House in Chicago, for four days starting July 21. Gibson certainly showed at least one Flying V – a photograph appeared in show coverage in the September number of *Piano Trade Magazine*. It showed Julius Bellson, Clarence Havenga, and Ted McCarty posing in front of a guitar display that included a Flying V. They probably had two Vs to hand, in fact: the day-book log reveals two Flying Vs marked for CMI, Gibson's parent company, rather than the usual dealer's name, which were shipped on June 5, well in time for the show. Gibson may have had an Explorer on hand to show visitors, too, although the photographic evidence suggests that the main display at the Gibson booth prominently featured a Flying V alone from the Modernistic line.

The Explorer was another unprecedented design. Its construction and general features were very similar to the Flying V: korina body and neck, white/black/white plastic pickguard; twenty-two-fret rosewood fingerboard with dot markers; scale length of twenty-four-and-three-quarter inches; control layout of two volumes, single tone, and pickup selector; and two humbucking pickups.

One apparent hangover from the 'Futura' style was that at least one Explorer seems to have been made with a split-V headstock, retained from the earlier design. However, Explorers in general had a new long, drooping headstock, which made the neck and headstock look something like an upside-down hockey stick. This pointy headstock, with a pearloid Gibson logo, was actually quite a practical design, and owed a little to the Fender head style, but its flamboyance added to the shockingly new look of the Explorer. It would later inspire the 'pointy' headstock of the popular superstrat design of the 80s. Gibson's Explorer had a conventional stop-tailpiece, unlike the V's special unit with its through-body stringing, and the jack, too, was conventionally situated on the bottom edge of the body.

The shape of the Explorer's body, however, was anything but conventional, and was perhaps even more radical than that of the Flying V. It's a pleasing mix of angularity and modern straight lines, with a wedge-shaped base and an elongated horn pushing out beyond the lower cutaway. It's balanced and assured, and another outstanding achievement from the design team at Gibson in the late 50s. The Explorer's shape and look would inspire many future guitar-makers and musicians, who would draw on and pay homage to this startling innovation from Kalamazoo. Gibson was convinced it was on to something. "Try one of these 'new look' instruments," insisted the original publicity. "Either is a sure-fire hit with guitarists of today!" Sadly, that was not the case. It was the guitarists of tomorrow who would make it a hit.

In Gibson's archive of 'day-book' logs from this period, there are no entries for any Explorers at all. This is not the result of some oversight at the time; it's because of a gap that appeared later in Gibson's archive. It's a gap that today drives guitar historians mad. The specific log that would show us all the details we need just does not exist. Others are there that log the serial numbers and shipping dates of virtually every instrument that left the factory around the classic period. However, the one that would cover the Modernistic models in most detail is missing.

Walter Carter, a former historian at Gibson, explains that the company's archive has two primary sets of records. The first set is the serial logs, and in these were recorded serial numbers of guitars as they were produced, in number order. The second set is the day-books, in which was recorded models and their serial numbers, in date order. There is also a third set, the shipping totals, where annual figures were reckoned up for each model.

"It's the day-books that are missing for this period, and in fact for all the solidbody models of that period," says Carter. "The other main set of books, the serial logs, go all the way through – but unfortunately they are for 'A' numbers only, the hollowbody serials, and not the solidbody ink-stamped numbers. What Gibson has is the day-books up to June 30 1958, the A-series hollowbody numbers complete, and the new 'impressed' numbers, for all models, in numerical order, beginning in 1961 and complete for the first few years. And there's no shipping log for the 60s."[20]

The best guess must be that the missing day-book, the one that would complete the picture of exactly which Modernistics were made and when and to whom they were shipped, has simply been lost. The only relevant existing day-book, the one that comes right before the missing one, ends abruptly on Monday June 30 1958. Up to that date it includes entries for 52 Flying Vs – but not one Explorer. The conclusion must be that Explorer production did not begin until at least the beginning of July.

Thankfully, the sheets do still exist where the factory manager would tally up each year's production. At the end of 1958, the Gibson man wrote "81" in the column for the total number of Flying Vs shipped that year. It seems like a small number, and it certainly pales when you consider it against the bestselling solidbody instruments shipped that year, which inevitably tend to be the cheaper models: the manager's tallies show 2,408 Les Paul Juniors and 958 Specials, 1,528 ES-125s and 1,522 ES-125Ts, and 2,005 ES-225Ts.

Several higher-price models sold worse than the $247.50 Flying V in 1958. Gibson shipped 61 Byrdlands in 1958, 49 ES-295s, 48 L-5CESs, 32 of the new double-necks, and just 30 Super 400-CESs (Gibson's most expensive electric model, which listed at $675 or $700 depending on finish). The V was a mid-price guitar, and the same-price Les Paul

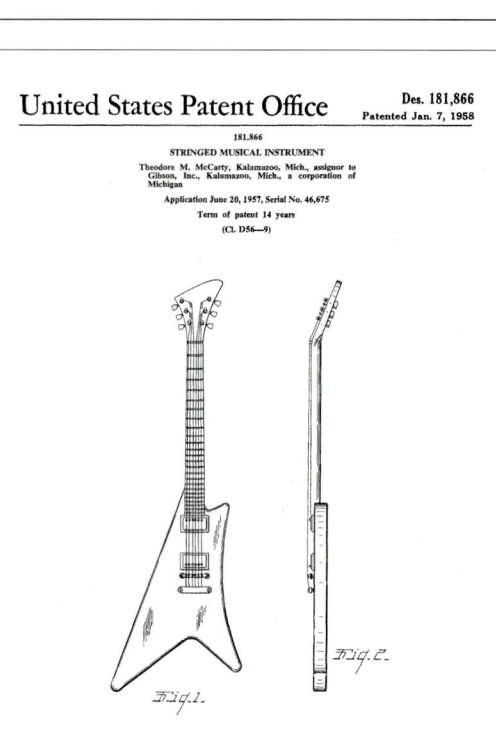
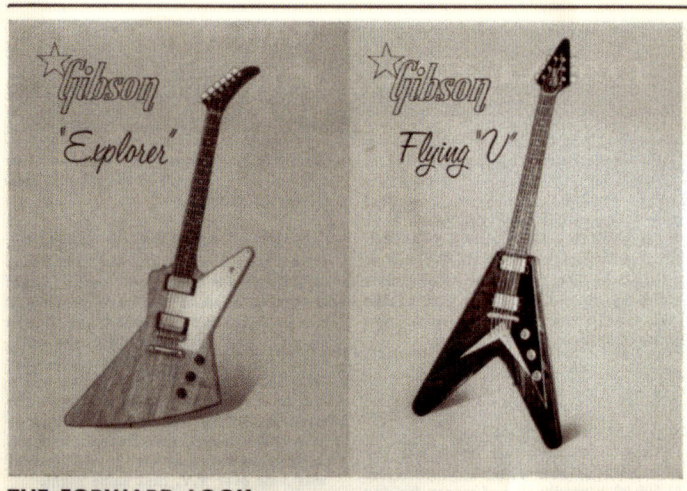

30 FLYING V ■ EXPLORER ■ FIREBIRD

MODERNISTIC FLOP

- The only picture of an Explorer in Gibson publicity came in the April–May 1958 issue of the **Gibson Gazette** (left), showing an Explorer, with its now standard pointy headstock, and a Flying V. And the only appearance on a **pricelist** came in July that year (centre, below). The **Moderne** (**patent**, far left) was a proposed third modernistic guitar that was taken no further at the time, although a 1992 **magazine hoax** (right) pretended that there was a peculiar fourth model, which it called the **Thunderbolt**.

	MODERNISTIC GUITARS	
Explorer	Guitar, Solid Body	$247.50
Flying V	Guitar, Solid Body	247.50
	Case for above models	75.00

- The Explorer has become one of the most sought-after collectables, because Gibson made only 22 examples in 1958 and '59. This **1958 Explorer** (main guitar) was sold by Eric Clapton at auction in 1999 for $134,500. Gibson assembled a few leftover Explorers and Vs until about 1963 and, as this **1962 Explorer** (top) shows, used period hardware. Some music stores used the Flying V in **window displays** (right), but Gibson had to accept its brave new designs were 50s failures.

FLYING V ■ EXPLORER ■ FIREBIRD

Goldtop, which morphed into the Sunburst-finish Standard during 1958, shipped 434 units – more than five times the Flying V figure.

The Explorer appears on the annual tally for 1958 as "Korina (Mod. Gtr)", and the number written in there is 19. There's no doubting that this is a pitifully small number, however you look at it. For 1959, the final entries for the original V and Explorer are lower still. Gibson shipped 17 Vs that year and just three Explorers. This collapse of interest in the Modernistic guitars must have been a huge disappointment.

About the only positive spin Gibson could put on this failure was that some enterprising store owners found the new instruments useful in window displays designed to attract potential customers. One example proudly presented in the September–October 1958 issue of the *Gibson Gazette* was the Scalise Music Center of Richmond, California, and its imaginative space-travel window theme, mounted just a few months after America's fourth satellite went successfully into orbit. The impressive display featured fanciful depictions of a rocket ship and a satellite alongside a real Flying V. "When the futuristic guitar arrived at their store," reported the *Gazette*, "it created such excitement among employees that Mr Weishahn, store manager, decided to use it alone in a window display. Public reaction was tremendous – never had there been such crowds around the windows."[21]

Apparently, that particular V was sold within two days. Other stores were less successful with the hard-to-sell new models, and while production stopped in 1959, some Vs and Explorers were certainly hanging around in shops into 1960 and sometimes well beyond. A few lonely-looking Vs turned up in store photos in later copies of the *Gazette*, including one at the Art Music Shop of Montgomery, Alabama, pictured in an issue dated January–February 1961. Later still, in 1962 and '63, Gibson assembled and sold a few of its leftover Explorers and Vs, mostly using contemporary fittings such as nickel-plated hardware and metal-capped knobs.

Marv Lamb, who began working for Gibson in 1956 in the wood shop, says: "I remember working on the Flying V and Explorer. They were the ugliest things, way ahead of their time. I think Gibson practically gave them away to get rid of them: they had them hanging around for years." He pauses, and then adds with a smile: "I wish now that I'd taken a few of them myself."[22]

What of the third model in the Modernistic series, the design that has become known as the Moderne? There's certainly no entry for one anywhere in Gibson's surviving logbooks, and the short answer is that the design probably never even got to prototype stage. Gibson's sole patent drawing in 1957 most likely marked the end of a very short road for this particular design. The late-'57 *Gazette* item that introduced the Flying V explained that Gibson, in coming up with its batch of new models, "investigated every conceivable idea – and a few inconceivable ones, too – used some, abandoned others, tried a few over again, and finally incorporated the best of these into the [line]".[23]

Ronald Lynn Wood attempted a longer answer to the question of the mythical third

Modernistic model in his 2008 book *Moderne: Holy Grail Of Vintage Guitars*. "I genuinely believe that in 1956 or 1957 at least one prototype Moderne was made," Wood tells me, "and it may or may not have been displayed the following year. What happened to that instrument is anyone's guess. Why would Gibson go through all that trouble to patent all three guitars and only prototype and display two of them? There certainly exist prototypes of the Flying V and the Explorer/Futura. Also, why would several different employees, including management, say they were made if it weren't true?"

Wood notes that surprising guitars do pop up from time to time. "It's very easy to discount things like that – one-offs, prototypes, and special guitars – without having proof. There are probably more gems hidden in the Kalamazoo area or in some collector's vault. Just because we haven't had the opportunity to view the instrument does not mean it isn't out there somewhere. I choose to believe an original Moderne is out there somewhere, waiting to come out of hiding."[24]

While I'd love nothing more than to see a genuine 50s Moderne appear, I can't be so optimistic. I've seen some of the questionable examples – Billy Gibbons of ZZ Top, a keen collector, tells me that of the two 'Modernes' he has, he knows one to be what he calls "an imitation" and would "prefer to reserve judgement" on the second[25] – but I've seen no evidence from back in the day that goes anywhere beyond the patent.

Gibson personnel and others have indeed recalled seeing a Moderne at the factory or at a trade show, but I know from my own interviews that memories are fallible, to say the least. Hardly surprising, given that we expect people to recall every event from the distant past in excruciating detail. And so, for example, one very high-up Gibson exec, who was right there in the thick of it at the time, told me that Gibson never produced a Sunburst-finish Les Paul in the late 50s. As far as a Moderne is concerned, with so much money waiting for a genuine original today, if one was out there, surely by now someone would have found it (and retired on the proceeds)?

Even the Moderne's name itself is a matter of doubt. The name does not appear anywhere in Gibson literature back in the day. It began to show up in print in the early 70s, possibly for the first time in Tom Wheeler's *The Guitar Book*, articulating the name that collectors were starting to use to describe the legendary non-model. "The Moderne was designed about the same time [as the Flying V and Explorer], but never mass assembled," Wheeler concluded in 1974.[26] "The Moderne is so rare that we have never even seen one," dealer George Gruhn wrote a year later.[27] The first official use of the Moderne name would not arrive until 1982, when Gibson applied it to a 'reissue' ... of a guitar that almost certainly never existed.

And that would be that for the original Modernistic guitars, were it not for one amusing postscript to this part of the story. We'll wind forward to 1992 for a moment, to a group of writers at the British *Guitar Magazine* who were busy deciding what to do for that year's April Fools item. It was a tradition among some journalists to feature a joke or spoof of some kind to mark this annual licence for stupidity. What followed from this apparently innocent jape is instructive about the vintage-guitar world of the early 90s.

A two-page feature appeared in the April 1992 issue of *Guitar Magazine* and was clearly a joke – or so you might have thought. Richard Chapman wrote about an example of the "Gibson Thunderbolt" turning up in Britain, saying that he "simply could not accept it" and worrying that he might have been "the victim of a hoax". The Thunderbolt was mischievously portrayed as an apparent fourth member of the original Modernistic set, with a body that looked as if the top half of a Flying V had been flipped forward, and with a double-V tailpiece in the shape of a lightning-bolt.

Chapman told a funny tale and peppered it with such unlikely characters as store-owner Hank Feaver of Electrifying Guitars in Memphis, who'd first sold this mythical guitar back in the 50s; Ted McCarty's cousin Fred, described as "Professor of Geometry at Michigan State University"; and the original owner, named as Dave Thompson but who "wants to remain anonymous". The final nudge in the ribs was the date for the guitar's supposed auction sale, which was given as April 1, or April Fools' Day as it's also known.

Alongside, Dave Burrluck wrote a fictional analysis of the guitar's playability. "From an ergonomic standpoint, the Thunderbolt is a joke," he said. Burrluck was one of the editorial team who came up with the ruse, along with Chapman, editor Paul Trynka, and Tim de Whalley, who created the mock-up instrument used to illustrate the feature. "It didn't play," recalls Burrluck of the dummy Thunderbolt. "I think Tim made the body by chopping up an oriental Flying V, and the neck was fixed on with a big screw sticking out of the back. Anyway, we hit the go button and got quite a bit of feedback. At first, most people got the joke. But then the silliness started."[28]

The first thing they noticed, says Burrluck, was André Duchossoir's *Gibson Electrics* book of 1994, which seriously noted the Thunderbolt as a model "recently given some exposure in England". Then they saw Rick Nielsen of Cheap Trick with an 'original' Gibson Thunderbolt. Today, Nielsen is amused when he recalls what happened. "I'd never seen one of those models before – I wonder why?" he smiles. "This dealer I knew from Florida, who'd probably seen the picture in the magazine but hadn't read the article, had actually put one together. He said hey, Rick, I'd like to show you something – and he told me it was the real deal, a Gibson Thunderbolt. He let me have it for a while, and it was actually quite a fun idea. But I've said it for years: a lot of guitar dealers remind me of used car salesmen, or pirates. You shouldn't trust them. But then who else wants to be in the business of dealing with musicians and crazy collectors? You have a little bit of pity for them … but not too much."[29]

In 1995, the Hamer company made Nielsen a Thunderbolt-style guitar, and Japanese maker Fernandes followed suit. Perhaps the strangest development in this strange tale of the model-that-never-was came in 1999, when Gibson's Custom Shop produced a couple of Thunderbolts for a trade show. Phil Jones, who worked at the Custom Shop for 15 years from 1984, explains how this happened. "I decided it would be the special project for the NAMM show that year. We'd always make something special, something unusual, to grab attention – I'd done a Super 400 fretless bass, for example," says Jones. "I liked the idea that the British magazine had done this to pull your leg, so I just thought what the heck. It's easy to reverse the two halves of a V body – and that's the Thunderbolt shape! It intrigued me, and so I made one in korina and one in mahogany for the show. It was something that started as a joke, and we went with it. It was a lot of fun."[30]

The Thunderbolt was a fabulous fabrication that enjoyed a remarkable journey, from April Fools fiction to Custom Shop fact in just seven years. It underlines how far we'll go in our need to believe that something might just be real – even if all the evidence points strongly in the other direction. "I suppose it's the ultimate accolade," chuckles Burrluck. "You invent a Gibson that never existed … and then Gibson makes one."[31]

Anyway, let's get back to the early 60s and a more reliable history. Gibson had survived what must have seemed like nothing more than an unfortunate blip in its sales plan, writing off the Flying V and Explorer as failed experiments and continuing forward into the new decade with a revised line of electric guitars. Double cutaways were definitely the in-thing, with the budget Les Paul models – Junior, Special, and TV – all adopting the new look by 1960. The shortlived Sunburst-finish Les Paul Standard, another future classic, was dropped from the line that same year following poor sales.

The news was better when it came to the ES-335, launched in 1958 as a development of the company's thin-body design that had started with the 'thinline' Byrdland and the ES-350T three years earlier. When it came to the new 335, however, Gibson deployed a double-cutaway design and a novel solid block within the otherwise hollow body, intended to create a new kind of semi-solid structure. It effectively combined a hollowbody guitar with a solidbody, not only in terms of construction but also in sonic effect, and by the early 60s, sales of this fine new instrument were growing steadily.

New ideas were filtering through to other models. Jimmie Webster at Gretsch in New York City originally investigated the prospects for a stereo guitar. He filed a patent for a stereo pickup system in 1956, leading to Gretsch's wonderfully named Project-O-Sonic guitars. Gibson's first take on the stereo idea, the ES-345, appeared in 1959, along with optional stereo wiring for the 355. Another new Gibson feature that aimed to assist the guitarist's search for fresh electric timbres was the Varitone control, offered on the 345 and some 355s. It allowed selection of one of six preset tone options, and in combination with the pickup selector expanded to 18 potential tonal shades. Gibson's Varitone and stereo capabilities were never especially popular among guitarists, who often disconnected the Varitone and, despite the stereo option, simply played what was a good guitar in conventional mono mode. At the other end of the electric line, Gibson launched in 1959 the Melody Maker, its first low-end solidbody aside from the Les Paul Juniors. By 1961, Gibson had decided on a complete makeover in an effort to try to reactivate its faltering

Les Paul models. During 1960, the company had started a $400,000 expansion at the factory, which more than doubled in size by the time the work was completed the following year. It was the third extension to the original 1917 factory following additions in 1945 and 1950. The latest single-storey brick-and-steel building resulted in a plant of more than 120,000 square feet that extended for two city blocks at Parsons Street in Kalamazoo. One of the first beneficiaries of the expanded production facilities was the completely revised line of Les Paul models. Gibson redesigned the Junior, Standard, and Custom, applying a modern, sculpted double-cutaway design at first using the Les Paul name, although during 1963 the firm began to call them the SG Junior, the SG Standard, and the SG Custom.

The same year saw Gibson introduce a completely new line of solidbody electrics, the Firebirds, with strong links back to the failed Explorer design. The motivation, again, seems to have been to compete with Fender's growing dominance of the solidbody market. "We wanted another deal, something that our friend Fender couldn't make," Gibson boss Ted McCarty told me later.[32] This time, in an effort to make something distinctive that would not be limited by traditional guitar forms, Gibson hired an outside designer to concoct something new and remarkable. And that's exactly what they got.

Ray Dietrich was a legendary car designer who had worked in the auto industry for 50 years. He'd started in the drawing office of a small firm in the 1910s, learning how coachbuilders worked from original drawings. In the 20s and 30s, Dietrich established the idea of the custom coachbuilder, who finalises a design on paper before it's manufactured. Based in New York City and then Detroit, Dietrich headed a number of firms, including his grandly named LeBaron Carrosiers, designing and building exclusive car bodies and working for makers like Lincoln, Packard, Duesenberg, and Ford. Two of his distinctive production designs were the stylish Reo Royale Eight of 1931 and the handsome Chrysler Airstream of 1935. After working as a consultant to the Checker Cab company, he founded Raymond Dietrich Inc in 1949 in Grand Rapids, Michigan. Four years later, Dietrich returned to consulting work for Checker, and in 1960, at the age of 66, he retired to Kalamazoo.

A few years into his retirement, Dietrich met Gibson boss Ted McCarty. McCarty went to a talk where Dietrich reminisced about his car designs, and afterward McCarty introduced himself and asked if Dietrich would be interested in designing a guitar. The result was that Gibson hired him to devise a new solidbody electric line. Dietrich eventually came up with a fantastic-looking design – but it still needed a name. "I was sitting in my office one day with Ray and a couple of the other fellas," McCarty recalled, "and we were trying to come up with a name for this thing. He said: why don't you call it Phoenix? Isn't that the firebird, I said, the old story of rising from the ashes? So that's where the name came from. And Ray also designed the firebird logo on the pickguard."[33] The new Firebird line appeared in the 1963 catalogue, and Gibson was ready to shout about it, proclaiming "this revolutionary new series of solidbody guitars. Exciting in concept, exciting to play. You'll find a whole new world of sound and performance potential … plus that sharpness in the treble and deep, biting bass. … A completely new and exciting instrument that offers all the sound, response, fast action, and wide range that could be desired".

There were four Firebirds, the I, III, V, and VII, each with different appointments but following the same overall design and build. (The two missing numbers II and IV were allocated to a pair of matching Thunderbird bass models; there was no VI.) Gibson announced the new line just before the 1963 NAMM show in Chicago and displayed them there in Rooms 826–829 at the Palmer House hotel from July 21–25. They first appeared on the July pricelist and production began about three months later.

The Firebirds were the first Gibson solidbody electrics to make use of a through-neck construction – all Gibsons had a glued-in set neck, while Fender used a screwed-on neck joint. Some guitar-makers felt that through-neck construction provided better sustain and tone. Rickenbacker was the only commercial maker to regularly employ a through-neck at the time, but it was not until a brief period around 1980 that it would become widely popular. For the Firebirds, a central multi-laminate mahogany-and-walnut section ran the entire length of the guitar, from headstock to strap button, providing the neck and the mid portion of the body in a single unit.

Two slightly thinner mahogany 'wings' were then glued on to complete the body shape, and as a result the mid portion of the body was stepped up a little higher than the wings, forming a sort of central shelf, four inches wide, on which the pickups, bridge, and tailpiece sat. The back of the body had a gentle contour at the top, another feature better known on Fender guitars and designed for player comfort.

The body shape was sleek and asymmetrical, coming on something like an Explorer with curves – there's no mistaking that angled parallelogram – although the Firebird was an altogether more exciting design. The elongated shape had a horn-less upper section that made the lower horn appear to stick out further than it really did. The result was an almost-unbalanced but quite appealing look, and it was this that led to these original models becoming known among collectors and players as the 'reverse body' or simply 'reverse' Firebirds.

There were twenty-two metal frets on a rosewood (I, III, V) or ebony (VII) fingerboard glued to the face of the neck, with binding on the III, V, and VII, over a channel in which sat a strengthening metal truss-rod. The adjustment nut for the rod was under a cover on the headstock. In the face of the fingerboard were position markers – small circular pearloid dots (I, III), large pearloid crowns (V), or large pearl blocks (VII) – inlaid in front of the first (VII only), third, fifth, seventh, ninth, twelfth, fifteenth, seventeenth, nineteenth, and twenty-first frets, with the twelfth-fret octave position marked on the I and III by a pair of dots. There were nine small corresponding position dots on the upper

● The new Firebirds debuted in 1963 plus a pair of matching Thunderbird basses (ad, top). This **1964 Firebird V** (main guitar) has the line's regular sunburst finish and unusual 'banjo' tuners. Gibson copied Fender's idea of **custom colours** (chart showing full line, top). This **1964 Firebird V** (opposite), for example, is finished in Ember Red.

38   FLYING V ■ EXPLORER ■ FIREBIRD

RISE OF THE FIREBIRD

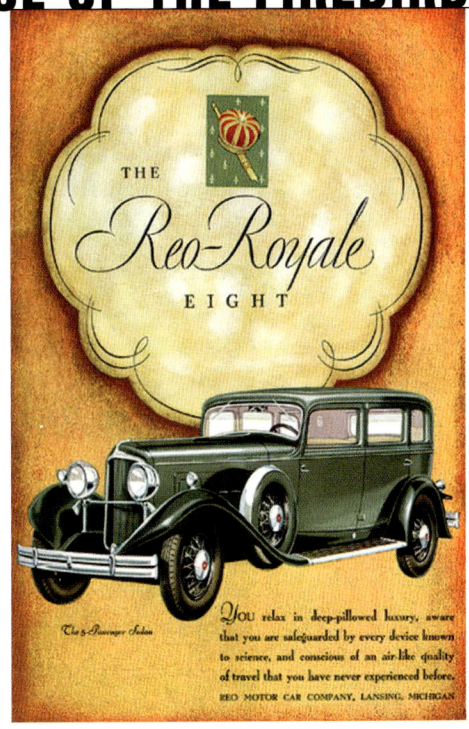

- **Ray Dietrich** was a renowned car designer whom Gibson hired to come up with a fresh look for a new solidbody electric. The result was the first **Firebird** line, now known as the reverse-body style thanks to the almost upside-down look of the body shape. Dietrich (pictured, above, in the 70s) designed car bodies for Lincoln, Packard, Ford, Duesenberg, and others, including the 1931 Reo Royale Eight (**Reo** ad, above). He retired in 1960, and a few years later met Gibson boss Ted McCarty, who persuaded Dietrich to design a guitar. This first Firebird style lasted until 1965.

FLYING V ■ EXPLORER ■ FIREBIRD

39

● Gibson soon realised its original Firebird guitars were expensive to build and in 1965 launched a revised design. This **1965 Firebird I** (above) in Polaris White and a **1966 Firebird III** (below) in Sunburst show the new look, with 'non-reverse' body, P-90 pickups on cheaper models, and a more conventional Fender-like headstock with standard tuners. Gibson disposed of the complex through-neck of the earlier type, relying instead on its typical glued neck. The new Firebirds lasted in the line until they too were dropped in 1969.

FLYING V ■ EXPLORER ■ FIREBIRD

FIREBIRD FLIPPED

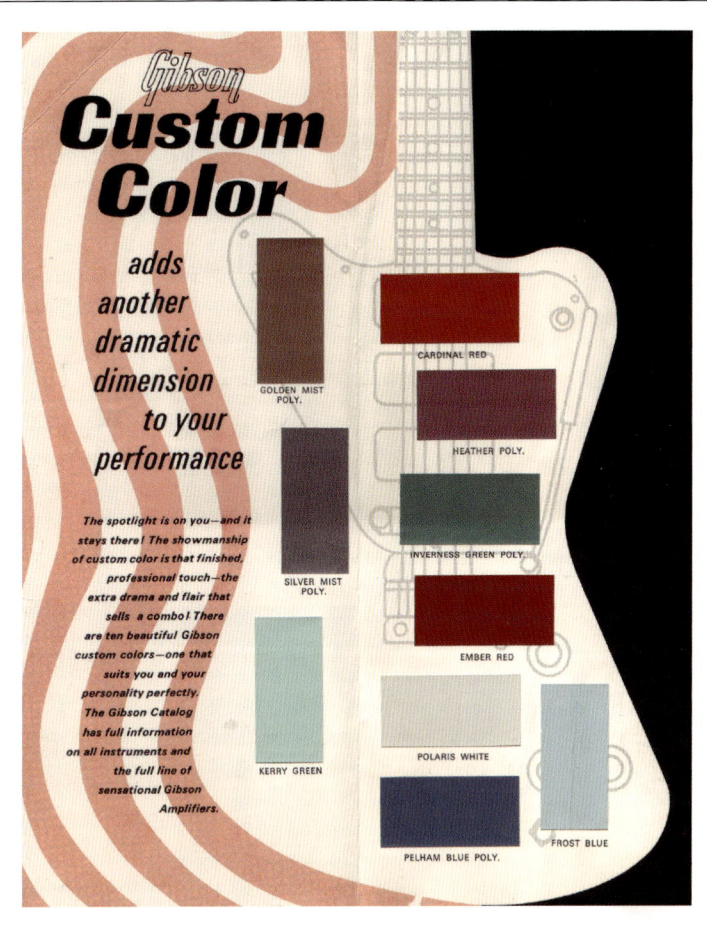

- Fender had noticed some similarities between the original 'reverse-body' Firebirds and its offset-body Jaguar and Jazzmaster models, and issued this **ad** (right) as a kind of public sign of its displeasure. When Gibson introduced its revised 'non-reverse' models, the new Firebirds were again offered in custom colours, and the company made another **colour chart** (above right) with ten swatches to advertise the feature. The colourful **1966 catalogue** (above) displayed a Firebird VII (left) finished in Frost Blue, a Firebird V (centre) in Kerry Green, and a Firebird III (right) in Cardinal Red.

FLYING V ■ EXPLORER ■ FIREBIRD

Metallic. Harrell reckoned that Pelham Blue and Cardinal Red were the two most requested custom Firebird finishes, after the much more popular regular Sunburst.

The July 1963 Zone 1 pricelist noted each of the Firebird models as a "New Style Guitar" and pitched their prices across the range: the I was listed at $189.50, the III at $249.50, the V at $325, and the VII at $445. There was an optional case, which added $46, while a custom colour – "choice of Duco colors for above models" – added just $15. The VII was Gibson's most expensive single-neck solidbody electric, listing $20 higher than a Les Paul Custom, while the least expensive Firebird, the I, sat a touch below the $210 SG Special of the time.

The Firebird models sold better than the Explorer ever did – that would hardly be difficult – with the two-pickup III the most popular. By the start of 1965, however, Gibson's factory managers were well aware of several problems. The Firebird was a difficult and expensive guitar to make, and it was becoming clear that employing an outside designer who did not understand guitar production could have its drawbacks.

In the factory, if a neck were to develop a fault, then the through-neck design meant that a good portion of the body, too, was lost at the same time. The intricacies of the laminate through-neck and the carving and the tricky wiring all added to production time and, therefore, costs. And once the Firebirds got out into the real world, they were unfortunately prone to breakages at the fragile junction where the head met the neck. Some of the breaks would occur while the guitar was still in its case, where the crucial part of the instrument was unsupported.

Gibson decided to pull the plug, and wound down production of these original Firebirds. At the same time, the company was devising new versions with simpler construction and a revised design. Over the years, the story that emerged from Gibson managers was that Fender had threatened to sue Gibson over the design of the original reverse Firebird design, citing Fender's existing offset-waist body, as used on the Jazzmaster and Jaguar models. It was said this was the reason Gibson was forced to change the first Firebird design, but this seems unlikely.

Fender was certainly annoyed, and published an ad at the time showing the Jazzmaster and Jaguar below a headline that reads 'The Most Imitated Guitars In The World'. But Fender had little scope for legal action. It had only a simple design patent for the Jazzmaster, granted in December 1959, and described the Jazz and Jag's Offset Contour Body as "patent pending". The story that Fender was the culprit may simply have been a convenient cover behind which Gibson could hide its financial and practical motives for changing the Firebird design.

The most obvious change to the line of brand new Firebirds that appeared in 1965 was a slightly more conventional body shape, looking as if the original had been flipped upwards and over. As a result, players and collectors refer to them now as the 'non-reverse' Firebirds, in contrast to the earlier 'reverse' body. Gone was the through-neck and the body 'shelf', replaced with Gibson's conventional glued-in neck. The pickups on the two cheaper models were regular P-90 single-coils, and the headstock was more Fender-like and came with regular tuners. Some transitional models mix reverse and non-reverse features.

The new Firebirds first appeared on the June 1965 pricelist, and a price-drop was immediately apparent. The final reverse Firebirds had listed at $500 (VII), $360 (V), $280 (III), and $215 (I), whereas the new non-reverse line was notably cheaper: $379.50 (VII), $289.50 (V), $239.50 (III), and $189.50 (I). Gibson briefly made a 12-string Firebird V, too, introduced in 1966. But the price-cut and design changes were not enough to stop a decline in sales of the non-reverse Firebird models during the 60s, and at the end of the decade they were finally dropped.

Meanwhile, some pioneering guitarists had taken up other pointy Gibsons, and the new interest in the Flying V in particular would prompt Gibson to reintroduce that model in modified form. Lonnie Mack and Albert King were two of the earliest players to recognise the lure of the V, and each seems to have acquired an original Flying V back around the time of the model's launch in the late 50s. Mack hit the big time in 1963 when his rousing instrumental cover of Chuck Berry's 'Memphis' took him and his Flying V into the Top Five in the US singles chart. He had his original guitar fitted with a Bigsby vibrato, which required an ungainly metal bar to be fitted across the legs of the V. Mack has always claimed that his V, which he named Number Seven, was the seventh off the production line.

Albert King, too, acquired his first Flying V soon after the model's original introduction in the late 50s. The left-handed King found the symmetrical V and its humbuckers a perfect fit for his stinging blues style, and he adapted a regular right-handed model for influential cuts such as his late-60s Stax single 'Born Under A Bad Sign'. King played a couple more versions of the V, including later a proper left-hander custom-built by the guitar maker and repairer Dan Erlewine.

Billy Gibbons has been in ZZ Top since the band's formation in 1970, but a few years earlier he had been personally introduced to the world of korina Gibsons. He was a member of The Moving Sidewalks, had been though a Jazzmaster and a Tele, and was currently playing a Strat, but he'd let it be known in and around Houston, Texas, that he was looking for a good Gibson with humbuckers. Word had filtered down that the tone of these pickups was something worth getting hold of. One day a friend, Reid Farrell, asked if he was still looking for one of those old guitars. Gibbons takes up the story. "I eagerly said yes man, what you got? I said it doesn't have to be a Les Paul necessarily, but I suspect it's something to do with those two big pickups. I didn't even know what they were called. He said well, I've got a guitar that has those pickups on it and I'll sell it to you."

The instrument turned out to be a 1958 Gibson Flying V – a guitar even rarer than a Sunburst Les Paul. "He brought it over. I said what *is* that? But I said I don't care, it's got those pickups. So I bought it for 300 bucks. And sure enough, man, we stepped up to the land of humbucking. It was really wicked. Hadn't really given humbuckers much

● **Albert King** is best known for his single 'Born Under A Bad Sign', and he was a fine blues guitarist. He used three Flying Vs, today owned by actor and blues fan Steven Seagal: original '59 Gibson (left and below left), a custom Dan Erlewine (centre), and a '67 Gibson (right).

● In the late 50s when Gibson launched its new Modernistic guitars, the Flying V and the Explorer, hardly any guitarists took much interest in what most of them saw as a couple of oddball designs. Nonetheless there were a few who saw something attractive in the V. Two of the most important early adopters are featured here: **Albert King** (above) and Lonnie Mack (opposite). King was a left-handed bluesman who found that the symmetrical body of the Flying V suited his style and his sound very well. This **70s Dan Erlewine Flying V** (main guitar) was custom built for King by guitar maker and repairer Erlewine, following on from a couple of earlier Vs that King played (see above).

46   FLYING V ■ EXPLORER ■ FIREBIRD

Vs FOR FREDDIE, LONNIE, BILLY

● **Lonnie Mack** (above) got an original **Flying V**, refinished red, in time for his 1963 hit 'Memphis'. It's owned today (right) by Cheap Trick's Rick Nielsen, who says Mack's Bigsby addition (jacket, above) was long gone. **Billy Gibbons** of ZZ Top played an original Flying V on their 1975 album *Fandango!* (top).

FLYING V ■ EXPLORER ■ FIREBIRD

47

thought, because I was on a Hendrix trail with my Strat, but here we were in the land of fat. That instrument stayed front and centre for, oh, a number of years, despite the fact that we later landed a Sunburst Les Paul, which I called Pearly Gates."[34]

Gibbons was the lucky recipient of something of a deluge of fine guitars: not only the V and his now-famous Burst, but also, in the mid 70s, an Explorer. The Les Paul got the most attention, but he did use the V and Explorer on stage from time to time – he points to ZZ Top's fourth album from 1975, *Fandango!*, the live side of which he says is full of V work. "The V had an interesting balance, so we kept on," he says. "And the picture of Albert King with his V started to appear, and we said gee whizz, this is an instrument of importance. I said if he liked it, we'd better like it."[35]

Brian Jones and Keith Richards did some satisfying shopping during 1965, when each of them acquired a sunburst-finish reverse Firebird VII. They performed a great twin-bird TV moment toward the end of that year when the Stones did 'Get Off Of My Cloud' on the US music show *Hullabaloo*, with an impressive Firebird either side of the stage. A year or so later, Jones got a non-reverse Firebird VII, which he played occasionally in the period before his death in 1969.

Dave Davies of The Kinks was the first well-known guitarist to be seen with an original korina Flying V in the 60s. Davies got his rare bird when the British band toured America in summer 1965. His regular Guild went missing en route to the West Coast at the end of June, and in a mad dash he had to get a new guitar in time for an appearance on the *Shindig!* TV programme. "When I flew to LA to do the show," Davies said in 1977, "my guitar was lost on the airline. I was heartbroken. So when we arrived in LA a guy said come along, I'll take you to a store, and we'll have a look around. And they had all these guitars, but I didn't like any of them. So I looked up on the top shelf and saw this dusty old case. I said: what have you got there?"[36]

Davies left the store with a significant prize: an original Flying V, presumably one of the neglected and unsold ones that had been lying around in stores like this for a good few years. He recalled later that it cost him about $200. It remained his favourite for some time, and it raised many an eyebrow among American and British guitar fans, not least because of the way the Kink would hook his right arm through the legs of the V's body in order to play it. A British magazine reported: "So many people have been enquiring about the weird guitar that Dave Davies has been using that [British distributor] Selmer has contacted Gibson to find out about it. It's called the Flying Arrow and was made for a specialty act in America. Gibson felt that it was too way-out to be a success, and it was only by luck that Dave happened to get his secondhand in the States. As yet, there is no possibility of it being put on the market."[37]

That was at the start of 1966. Soon, however, plans were under way at Gibson to launch a new version of the Flying V, and in October *The Music Trades* magazine reported: "Unprecedented demand for old models of the Gibson Flying V guitar has caused the company to put the famous instrument back into production. Since Gibson discontinued the Flying V it has virtually become a collectors item in England and Europe."[38] The reworked model featured different hardware and materials compared to the original late-50s V. It didn't have the through-body stringing or body-edge rubber strip, but it gained a large white pickguard and truss-rod cover, a mahogany body and neck, a Tune-o-matic bridge plus Gibson Maestro Vibrola vibrato, and chrome-plated hardware.

Gibson redesigned the control layout, too, now arranging the three familiar knobs – two volumes and a tone – into a triangular group rather than the three-in-line style of the original, providing the new Flying Vs with a quickly identifiable look. The revised model retained the overall body and headstock shape, with some minor tweaks, and kept the regular scale-length, the 22-fret rosewood board with dot markers, and the all-important pair of humbucking pickups, now integrated into the pickguard.

In their 2007 book *Gibson Flying V*, Zachary R. Fjestad and Larry Meiners suggest that Gibson made five batches of these late-60s Flying Vs, with 35 guitars in each, totalling 175 instruments shipped: two in 1966 (probably samples), 111 in 1967, none in 1968 (probably because Gibson was busy that year reissuing another solidbody model, the original single-cut Les Paul), 15 in 1969, and 47 in 1970. The new Flying V first appears on the October 1966 pricelist at $325 in Sunburst and an extra $20 for Cherry finish, and the final appearance is on the June '68 list, where the price has risen slightly to $375, in Sunburst, Cherry, or Sparkling Burgundy. The revised V is not featured in any of Gibson's catalogues of the period, nor in the promo magazine *Gibson Gazette*. It's almost as if the model was an indulgence afforded little importance within the company.

Jimi Hendrix thought otherwise. Of course, he was best known as a Fender Stratocaster player, but in 1967 Jimi acquired one of the revised-design Flying Vs. Nearly 30 years later, a British musician, Dave Brewis, rediscovered Hendrix's actual guitar. The story of how he found it is enough to keep every guitar nut digging around for that out-there-somewhere dream guitar.

Brewis, who lives in north-east England, had always been a Jimi fan, but he started collecting Hendrix gear in the mid 90s, specifically as the result of an auction where he first bought some amps and effects. "The kind of normal things you'd find in a musician's garage: they were all there," he says, but among the guitars a Sunburst Flying V stood out. "That started me wondering where the psychedelic one was." He's referring to the 1967 Flying V that Hendrix played as his main blues guitar for around half his career – an important number-two guitar to his primary Strats. It's known as the psychedelic V because, soon after he got it, Hendrix painted its body with some colourful decorations of his own devising. Nothing had been seen of this distinctive instrument since Hendrix's death in 1970.

Brewis did little more than wonder about it until he visited a local guitar store, where the owner happened to mention he'd just taken a 'Hendrix Flying V' in a part-exchange

● **Jimi Hendrix** (above) used this **1967 Flying V** (main guitar) from summer 1967 to early '69 as his main guitar for blues numbers. Guitarist Dave Brewis rediscovered the instrument years later and restored the psychedelic body painting that Hendrix had added. The main guitar has the V with Brewis's first attempt at the artwork, and the snaps (above right) show a couple of stages in the restoration process. Hendrix used a couple more Vs: a sunburst V, and then a custom black **left-handed V** seen at the Isle Of Wight festival in 1970 (left).

FLYING V ■ EXPLORER ■ FIREBIRD

ONE PAINTED WISH

● Gibson's new-style Flying V of 1967 was a more popular and widely-used guitar than the original. Among the players who found the revised instrument to their liking was **Marc Bolan** of T.Rex (above right), whose **1968 Flying V** is shown here (top centre), pictured for its auction sale in 2007.

FLYING V ■ EXPLORER ■ FIREBIRD

55

by a number of strikes in the 60s, including a 16-day stoppage in 1966. Gibson president Ted McCarty and his number two, John Huis, left that year after purchasing the Bigsby musical accessories company of California, which they re-established in Kalamazoo. In February 1968, after a number of short-stay occupants in the president's chair, Stan Rendell was appointed president of Gibson and set about his task of improving the company's fortunes.

"One of the reasons I was hired was because Gibson's electric sales were floundering," says Bruce Bolen. "About all we had in solidbody electrics were SGs, plus the archtop and thinline instruments, and they weren't selling all that well. The mainstay of the company at the time was the flat-top acoustics. So I was hired basically to go out and sell electric guitars."[41] The blues-rock boom at the time highlighted Gibson's obsolete single-cutaway Les Pauls as ideal instruments for the sound that players such as Eric Clapton and Michael Bloomfield wanted, and Gibson decided to reintroduce some of those old-style Les Pauls, launching them at the June 1968 NAMM trade show in Chicago. Bolen soon found himself out on the road promoting the 'new' Goldtop and Custom models. But he had other plans, too.

"I felt this little vibe," says Bolen, "that the world would like to see the Flying V and the Explorer and, eventually, even the Moderne. My intention originally was to reintroduce the '58 version of the Flying V, with korina wood, the Cadillac tailpiece, the slide-stopper on the rim, and all that good stuff." That plan was thwarted when the batch of korina Gibson ordered turned out to be badly streaked and unusable for a natural-finish instrument. "I'd already put this model into a production schedule and plan, so I decided we'd carry on with a limited edition, another variation of a V. I came up with the medallion concept, to indicate that it was a limited edition."

This 1971-only model was very similar to the '67-type V, with triangular control layout, large pickguard, and mahogany body. The main differences were the absence of a vibrato and the presence of period-specific Gibson details such as a volute, a sort of rear lump where headstock meets neck, designed to strengthen this weak spot, and "Made In USA" stamped into the rear of the headstock. Most obvious, visually, was a small circular metal medallion on the top of the upper leg of the V. Each medallion was marked with a Gibson logo and "Limited Edition Model" and was individually numbered.

"It was the first limited-edition series that Gibson did," says Bolen. "Limited editions intrigued me in other fields, especially guns, as shooting is one of my hobbies. Limited-edition guns would sometimes have the details imprinted or stamped into the metal of the barrel, so I transferred that idea to a guitar."[42] Gibson's shipping logs suggest a total of 350 medallion Flying Vs were produced in 1971. A year later, Bolen instigated a reissue of the 1963–65 reverse Firebird V. This, too, had an identifying limited-edition medallion on the body, just above the neck pickup, and was made in a similar quantity to the medallion V.

Gibson's ownership changed in 1969 when Norlin Industries was formed with the merger of its parent company, CMI, with ECL, an Ecuadorian brewery. They arrived at the Norlin name by combining the first syllable of ECL chairman Norton Stevens's name with the last syllable of that of CMI founder Maurice Berlin. Norlin was in three businesses: musical instruments, brewing, and 'technology'. The takeover was formalised in 1974 and Berlin, a man respected in the musical-instrument industry, was moved sideways in the new structure, away from the general running of the company.

Many people who worked at Gibson at that time feel there was a move away from managers who understood guitars to managers who understood mass-manufacturing. Some of the instruments made during the period soon after Gibson was taken over have a bad reputation today. The new owners are generally felt now to have been insensitive to the needs of musicians. It was a sign of the times. Economic analysts advised big corporations to diversify into a range of different businesses, pour in some money, and sit back to wait for the profits. There was a shift in emphasis toward the rationalisation of production, and this meant that changes were made to some Gibson guitars built during the 70s (and, to some extent, into the 80s). Generally, these alterations were made to save money, to limit the number of guitars returned for work under warranty, and to speed up production.

Meanwhile, there was still the occasional rare sighting of a 50s Gibson korina guitar. Keith Richards acquired an original Flying V in summer 1969 and played it at the Stones concert in London's Hyde Park in July, the famous event that took place just days after Brian Jones died. Perhaps Richards bought it specially for the gig? He appears not to have used it much again, although it did turn up at some of the sessions for *Let It Bleed*. It was among a few guitars stolen in 1971 from Villa Nellcôte, his temporary residence on the Côte d'Azur in France.

Grover Jackson grew up in Chattanooga, Tennessee, and was soon playing guitar in and around the state. As we'll discover later in the book, he went on to head the Charvel Jackson guitar company, which dominated 80s electric guitar design, but it was his experiences as a guitarist, vintage dealer, and fledgling guitar-maker in 70s Tennessee and then California that provided the background to that success. He soon got the korina bug, and recalls owning probably three original Vs and two Explorers. It was quite the exclusive club. "If you were interested in The Good Stuff," he says, "then the people in the know were few and far between, and everybody knew everybody else."

For Jackson that meant GTR in Nashville, an early version of vintage dealer Gruhn Guitars and a noted hang-out for a small band of guitarists-in-the-know. One of the things they knew about was that Albert and Lonnie played Flying Vs, but there was also this other pointy thing called an Explorer – which no one had seen. In 1970, however, Jackson received some important intelligence. He'd become friendly with Duane Allman and Berry Oakley of The Allman Brothers Band down in Georgia. "We're talking about guitars one day, and Duane tells me there's a guy playing with Leon Russell who's got this pointy guitar thing. Duane says: 'If I could get a guitar like that, I'd give you five thousand dollars for it.' Well, in those days, you might just as well have said five million dollars."

A few weeks later, Joe Cocker's Mad Dogs & Englishmen tour – with Russell as bandleader – played Atlanta, where Jackson was living. He casually bullshitted his way backstage and marched up to rhythm guitarist Don Preston. Preston did indeed play that rarest of prizes, an actual 50s Gibson Explorer, one of the original 22 that Gibson made. "In a fit of entrepreneurial genius, I said hey, I'll give you $2,500 for that guitar! And I didn't need a scientific calculator: I'm going to make out like a bandit here, right? But he wouldn't sell me the guitar," says Jackson, laughing at the memory. "That was the first Explorer I had ever seen. I distinctly remember asking where he got it, and he said he bought it out of a music store in Phoenix, Arizona."[43]

It seemed that Gibson hit at the right time with the revised Flying Vs, and a number of guitarists were drawn to the playability and visual appeal of the new version. Andy Powell joined Wishbone Ash with Ted Turner in 1969 to spearhead the band's impressive twin-guitar frontline, playing a homemade guitar on the British band's first album and a Gibson SG Special on the second. Then, Powell heard that the Orange store in London had a couple of late-60s Cherry-finish Flying Vs in stock. He knew about Flying Vs from a picture on a friend's Albert King album and from seeing Dave Davies of The Kinks playing one on the British TV chart show *Top Of The Pops*. "I distinctly remember that Dave played his up high, with his arm crooked into the V," says Powell, "which was a pretty impossible playing position."

Powell got down to Orange to see what was going on. "They had two identical Vs – and both still in the cardboard packing cases, despite this being 1972, about five years since they were made. No one had been interested in them, and I think they'd come over from the States. They were in mint condition," he recalls, "brand new and unplayed. As soon as I played the one I eventually bought for £300, I knew it was a great guitar."

Powell found the '67 V similar in feel to his SG, but he liked the way the V's humbuckers seemed brighter and more open-sounding than the SG's P-90s. "It really rang out acoustically, even before being amplified. I knew from my experiments with making instruments that this was a good sign. Also, crucially, it had a vibrola. I'd always liked a guitar with a whammy bar from my days playing tunes by The Shadows, and I found that if you used this particular unit gently it was a great effect, especially on open sustained chords – like the part I would play under the verse in 'Warrior' from our *Argus* album."

He took the guitar home to his bedsit in West Hampstead, north-west London. "I lay on the bed marvelling over what I had in my possession," he recalls. "As I looked at it resting on its two 'legs', up on a chair at the end of my bed, I couldn't believe I was the owner of such an exotic instrument."

Meanwhile, Wishbone Ash were growing as a popular act in the early 70s, with 1973's *Wishbone Four* hitting the US Top 50. "I started to identify even more with my guitar," says Powell. "It took on my mojo and I took on its mojo. Unlike Albert King, who made his Flying V look like a toy resting on his belly, I was a skinny eight-and-a-half-stone kid and the V was a big instrument for me, so I would wrap myself around it, sort of balancing it on one knee. It was a pretty unusual live playing style." Later, in London, Powell had a special violin-style v-shaped case made for his guitar, and it travelled all over the world with him. "The shaped case drew some pretty strange stares from customs guys and baggage handlers at airports," he reports. "I remember one guy in the States, down south in Texas somewhere, asked me if it was a snake catcher."

Powell has already mentioned Wishbone Ash's *Argus* album of 1972, and it was this record that had really put his band on the map. "You can hear my V all over the albums at that time," he says. "I did the majority of the guitar solos on *Argus* and the guitar simply sings on tracks like 'Throw Down The Sword' and 'Blowin' Free'. I would typically use it through two Fender tweed Concert amps, with four ten-inch Jensen speakers apiece, and no pedals. That was all you'd need. I got a clean ringing tone, which is the trademark of Wishbone Ash."

Later, Powell acquired a couple of original 50s Vs, and he found them quite different. "They had massive necks coupled with tiny, almost mandolin-type frets. They had an amazing sound, though, due to the lightweight korina wood, and they really rewarded the player." He's had three custom Royale mahogany-body Vs with extra piezo bridge pickups built since 2003 by the Welsh maker Kevin Chilcott, and Chilcott restored a white early-70s Gibson V that now "plays better than ever," Powell reports. "Recently, designer and luthier Jon Case has built me a really outlandish V called a JV1. I love working with luthiers like Kevin and Jon, which I think probably stems from my days attempting to build instruments."

How about the general complaint that you can't sit down and play a Flying V? "I've never found it to be a problem," Powell smiles. "But I've been playing them for so long, I just don't notice the issues that other guitarists might have. Overall, I wouldn't change anything on my 60s-style Vs. Maybe it's the mahogany one-piece body, featuring those wings, but it's a guitar that's just very vibrant and really sustains."[44]

Kim Simmonds in the British blues band Savoy Brown played a '67-style Flying V, and guitarist Marc Bolan also discovered the charms of the new 60s-style V. With his band T.Rex, Bolan had a run of UK hits in the 70s with his simple and effective pop guitar at their heart. He probably acquired his '68 V around the end of 1971, debuting it during the band's Electric Warrior tour that autumn. He also used it the following summer when T.Rex appeared on the British chart show *Top Of The Pops* miming to 'Get It On', their third Top Five single in a row. Bolan's Flying V wasn't in evidence after that, and it's likely he'd tired of the guitar, no matter how much it suited his increasingly

● Guitarist **Andy Powell** (below) of Wishbone Ash discovered the charms of the revised-design Flying V in the early 70s. He used his **1967 Flying V** (main guitar) for many classic Wishbone albums and on live dates (in 1973, below left).

62

FLYING V ■ EXPLORER ■ FIREBIRD

WISHBONE V

- Another influential V player is **Michael Schenker**, who at first used a '67-style Gibson with UFO and then his own bands. Today he plays a Dean (seen in 2007, right) that duplicates the distinctive black-and-white finish of his original.

- **Andy Powell** has played several other Flying Vs aside from his original Gibson. They include three custom **Royale Angel** Vs (number 3 seen on-stage in 2010, left) and a **Case** APJV (pictured above) with distinctive buckeye burl top. Another British player from the early 70s who took up Gibson's revised '67-style V was **Kim Simmonds**, pictured (right) with his band Savoy Brown at the Plumpton festival in 1970.

FLYING V ■ EXPLORER ■ FIREBIRD

From the start, Downing found Flying Vs to be comfortable, playable guitars. "They're essentially well balanced, and my first one was a light guitar," he says, "and totally great to play. Of course, there's been lots of various Vs and styles and shapes since then, and it's become *the* heavy metal guitar, really, with its pointy edges, the V and especially the later variations of it. Those original Vs we've been talking about are sort of softer looking, but now the more pointy jagged-edge razorblade look has become synonymous with metal. It just looks so aggressive!"[46]

What of the other Gibson pointy designs? Who was playing those in the 70s? It's not surprising that the Explorer was hardly seen at all, simply because it was such a rare guitar and almost nobody had heard of it, let alone actually owned one to play. Even so, Bill Spooner of The Tubes sometimes used an Explorer or a V amid his band's onstage mayhem, while Mick Ralphs could be seen occasionally with a V or Firebird with Mott The Hoople and sometimes a V, later, with Bad Company.

The Firebird was easier to come by, although hardly a front-runner among the Strats and Les Pauls and Teles more widely seen in the hands of the most prominent guitarists of the day. Eric Clapton had bought a reverse Firebird I in Philadelphia in April 1968 and used it during the Cream farewell concerts later that year. The bluesman Clarence 'Gatemouth' Brown played a modified non-reverse Firebird V for years, and in the 70s he was reaching a wider audience thanks to the blues revivals. Allen Collins probably played a Firebird on the long solo on the curiously over-rated 'Free Bird' (although Gary Rossington, who played slide on the track, insists that Collins used an Explorer), which Lynyrd Skynrd recorded for their first album, released in 1973.

However, one name stands out among early adopters of the Firebird: Johnny Winter, the great bluesman raised in Texas who, in 1969, was an early blues-rock signing to Columbia Records. Guitarists were well aware of his great slide playing and in awe of the gorgeous tone he drew from his Firebird. "I hadn't thought about buying one of those," Winter says of his first Firebird, which he got from dealer Ed Seelig. He'd played a variety of guitars before that, including Fenders and an SG. "I think I'd seen Firebirds, but before I got mine from Ed I'd never played one. I'm not sure where I was, but Ed was travelling to different festivals, and I saw it. I played it and liked the way it looked and sounded, so I bought it. It was either 1970 or '71 when I bought it for $225 cash."

Winter had a few more Firebirds, but that first one is the most famous, and remains his personal favourite. It's a Sunburst-finish 1963 reverse Firebird V, and pretty soon Winter replaced the vibrola with a regular tailpiece. "That's the one I play now," he says today. "I had another brown one, a white one, and red, green, and purple. I still have all six of them. The red one has an SG headstock on it, because it had been broken before I bought it. But that first one I ever bought is my favourite, because I've played it for so long and I've gotten used to it. They all sound different, but that one sounds the best. The neck is nice and thin, which I like, and it's not particularly heavy like a Les Paul. Of course, I wouldn't play it if I didn't like it," he laughs. "No, there's nothing it can't do. It's a great guitar."

Winter's taste for unusual Gibsons stretched to a Flying V at one point. "I really liked it because it was so different looking," he recalls. "It sounded real bassy and not as trebly as I like, but that one was stolen from me, I think at Toad's in New Haven, Connecticut." Another oddity is his Lazer guitar, a headless and tiny-body instrument that was built by Texan maker Erlewine. When we spoke during his 2010 tour, Winter used the '63 Firebird for two songs where he played slide and the Lazer for the rest of the show. His taste for the unusual doesn't seem to have been interrupted by too much philosophising. "I just think the Firebird is a cool shape," he says. "You never know what makes a guitar sound good. It could have something to do with the shape, but if it does, I certainly don't know about it."[47]

Phil Manzanera found himself in a completely different strand of rock music from Winter's energised blues, but he too saw the attraction of Gibson's striking Firebird design. "When I joined Roxy Music," he recalls, "I had a 335, and they sort of laughed when they saw it and said, well, that doesn't really go with the Roxy image: you have to get a Strat." Manzanera replaced guitarist David O'List in Roxy in 1972 and immediately got to work helping the British band develop a brilliant mix of rock'n'roll and art-rock, alongside vocalist Bryan Ferry and noise generator Brian Eno. At first Manzanera dutifully got a white Strat – "Eno's milkman had sold it to him for £30 and he sold it to me for £70" – and played it, together with his 335, on their first album.

Early in '73, however, he saw an intriguing small-ad in *Melody Maker*. "It said red Gibson Firebird, £160, 'owner leaving the country' or something. I thought hmm, a red guitar. The first guitar I ever bought, when I was sort of living in South America, was from Bell's shop in Surbiton, England, a red Hofner Galaxie. I thought: red guitars and rock'n'roll – that's got to be the business. I didn't have a visual clue about what a Firebird was. The ad did have the word Gibson in it, though, and all Gibson guitars were pretty expensive in those days."

Manzanera arrived at the owner's address, a big house in a posh part of London. "It turned out to be a young American teenager whose parents lived in this rich house. He opened the door and there it was: he was holding the red Firebird. I took one look at it and said that's for me! It looked like the flashest guitar ever. I didn't plug it in or anything – it could have not worked – but it was thank you very much, 160 quid, and I walked off with it." He'd landed a 1964 reverse Firebird VII in Cardinal Red. "It looked like the fins on the back of a Chevy or a Thunderbird, so it had to have American car colours."

It was the look that first appealed, and the guitar made an early visual appearance on the inner sleeve of the band's second album, *For Your Pleasure*. But Manzanera needn't have worried about the guitar's playability and sonic efficacy. "What transpired was that it was a wonderful recording guitar, because it seemed to fit within a perfect frequency

● **Johnny Winter** (above) has played his reverse-body **1963 Firebird V** (main guitar) since he bought the used instrument for a few hundred dollars back in the early 70s. The great bluesman found that the vibrato fitted to the original guitar was not to his taste, so he had that removed and fitted a regular bridge – the holes are still clearly visible on the body. Winter still uses the guitar today, primarily for slide work. He's used other Firebirds and other brands and models, but this original '63 remains a firm favourite.

FLYING V ■ EXPLORER ■ FIREBIRD

WINTER, SKYNYRD, AND KK

● A rare sighting (above) of an original Explorer, played by Lynyrd Skynyrd guitarist **Allen Collins** on-stage in 1977. **KK Downing** of Judas Priest is pictured (right) with his collection of Vs. He's holding his original and prized '67 Gibson (left) and a Mini V made by Hamer for the band's mid-80s Turbo tour. Against the wall at the back is an ESP made for the 90s Jugulator tour. Downing is pictured on-stage (top right) in 2009 with his latest V, a signature model by KxK.

FLYING V ■ **EXPLORER** ■ **FIREBIRD**

FLYING V ■ EXPLORER ■ FIREBIRD

RED BIRD AT THE ROXY

- **Phil Manazanera** used this Cardinal Red **1964 Firebird VII** (main guitar) with Roxy Music; he's pictured with it on tour in 1973 (opposite) and from the jacket of *For Your Pleasure* (right) that same year. Another Firebird fan was **Stephen Stills**, seen (above) with a Firebird I on stage in 1974. Around that time, **Hamer** started as a brand influenced by classic Gibson designs, including the Explorer. Hamer's **Jol Dantzig** (top) works on a new model with Ratt's **Robbin Crosby**, and in the Hamer workshop (centre) the Standard model takes shape.

FLYING V ■ EXPLORER ■ FIREBIRD

71

Goldtops and replacing them with flame tops, to make '59 Les Paul Standard replicas from real guitars," Dantzig recalls. "Some people would say counterfeiting, but at the time I don't think Jim really thought of it that way." Beach would do his milling openly, right in his shop, and honestly advertised that he could convert your Goldtop to a Burst.

Beach was tempted to make an Explorer copy, too. "He made a couple," recalls Dantzig, "and we purchased one from him. We learned from that, and we put a maple top and binding on it. We considered it a melting-pot, a hybrid approach, where we wanted to put the attributes of a Les Paul Standard and an Explorer together. We had a reverence for these designs."[53]

Jim Beach was not alone in building what are politely called conversions or replicas. Many guitar makers put their hand to such work, and the results depend on your point of view. If you've been stung by a guitar that looks like a real collectable but turns out to be a fake, you'll be inclined to see this as a murky business. If you paid less for something that's very close to the real guitar you want but can't afford, you'll be happy that such craftsmen exist. A replica may start life as a legitimate instrument, but if it has Gibson on the head and has been nowhere near that company's factories, later owners may be tempted to present it as something other than its true self.

One of the most renowned builders of replicas is Peter 'Max' Baranet, who was active in California from the early 70s to the late 90s. "People have the idea I was mass-producing replicas all my life," says Baranet. "They're actually very scarce. There are way less than a hundred – and that includes Flying Vs, Explorers, Strats, Teles, and Les Pauls. The reputation that I've got is out of proportion." There are no intentional marks on his guitars to identify them to the unwary as made-by-Max. "But if you're in the business of buying six-figure guitars and you can't tell that one of mine is not the real thing, you're in the wrong business," he insists. "They were great guitars, but they were never built to pass as real."[54]

Meanwhile, back in Chicago, Dantzig and Hamer would routinely go along to the big rock shows that regularly rolled into Chicago, finagle their way backstage, and hawk their vintage guitars. Now they had their hybrid Explorer-dressed-as-a-Les-Paul to show off, too. "We didn't want to sell it, actually," says Dantzig. "It was more like a way that we could differentiate our shop from other people: hey, look, check out what we're doing, we're cool. It was a way of bonding with our clients, showing them that we weren't just a couple of kids who had some guitars and stuff – we were serious about this. So we'd also show them our Explorer with the maple top."

This was how the Hamer brand began. The Explorer with the maple top morphed into the first Hamer model, the Standard. The operation began with four partners: Paul Hamer, Jol Dantzig, John Montgomery, and Montgomery's apprentice Jim Walker. Dantzig is clear in his memory about the new firm's debt to Gibson's Modernistic guitars. Gibson, based in Michigan, could hardly help absorbing the design culture around them.

"It was that futuristic mid-century look, a post-war look-at-us vibe: we've got jets with swept-back wings, cantilevered architecture, and the cars with tailfins coming out of Detroit – it was a combination of all those things."

Around this time, Hamer and Dantzig decided to visit the source. They drove to Kalamazoo to see Ted McCarty, who as we've seen had left Gibson and was now heading his own Bigsby company. "I'd seen Ted's signature on the patent of the Flying V and the Tune-O-matic tailpiece, and so, naturally, like many people, I assumed he was the person who actually designed them. In my mind, he was some kind of genius guitar guy. We took a Standard, our homage to the Explorer, to show him. It was like: look dad, look what we made," laughs Dantzig.

"He was really quite nice. But he took one look at it and said, you know, guitars like that are failures." Hamer and Dantzig wanted to say no, Ted, you were ahead of your time! "We wanted to say we're breaking out of the mould of Wes Montgomery and Les Paul, and this design is perfect for today's angular music. But he just wasn't interested at all in guitars. He really wasn't a guitar guy. It was a job: he was an executive, a businessman. He was really stoked about his new product, a flashlight called Flexlite, a little less about Bigsby, and even less about what had happened at Gibson and in the guitar industry. We left feeling demoralised in a certain way."

Dantzig and Hamer knew that the time of the pointy guitar design was upon them. "Ten, fifteen years since those original Vs and Explorers, these designs had become for some musicians like a badge of rebellion, taking a stand in opposition to what had come before, in an attempt to lay claim to some new sonic territory. 'I'm not Kenny Burrell, I'm not your grandpa's music; I've got my Marshall on 11 and I'm wearing platform shoes, and … check out this guitar!' And we got our guitars to the biggest bands in the world."

Dantzig reels off the names of early customers who bought the Standard, Hamer's souped-up Explorer. The first one went to Martin Barre of Jethro Tull; another went to Mick Ralphs of Bad Company; more to Rick Nielsen and Robin Zander from Cheap Trick. "We showed one to the guys in Thin Lizzy – they plugged in the guitar and suddenly it was wow! With that design, the soundboard is so huge. It's a thin guitar that's very, very broad, and that soundboard is so interactive when you have it cranked up through a big amplifier. It really sounds great! That was one of the most exciting things about the guitar. Anyway, by 1976, I was looking at all these people buying guitars from us, and I thought, well, this has probably got a bigger future than trying to buy stuff from a pawn shop, clean it up, and make a few hundred dollars on it."

Hamer went on to become a brand that did many things which guitarists thought Gibson should have been doing. The Sunburst model, launched in 1977, took the souped-up idea further, morphing a Les Paul Burst, a Telecaster, and a Les Paul Junior into a new, attractive, and playable whole. More followed, with the occasional pointy look thrown in: the X-shape GT model, designed for Judas Priest's Glenn Tipton in 1984

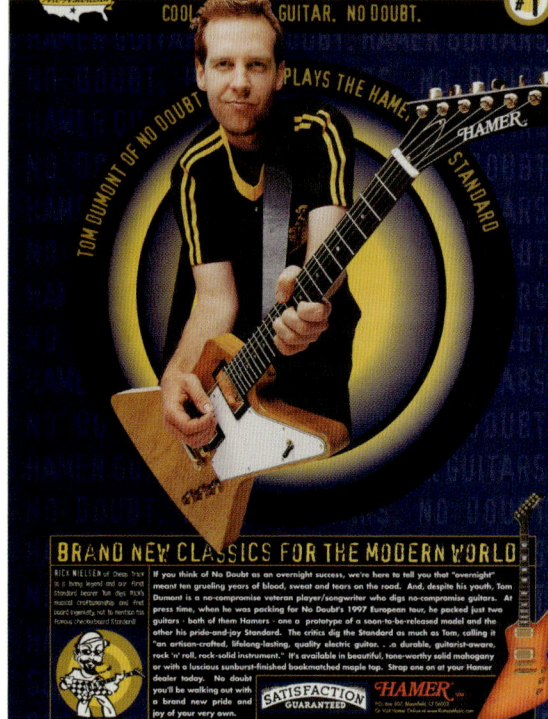

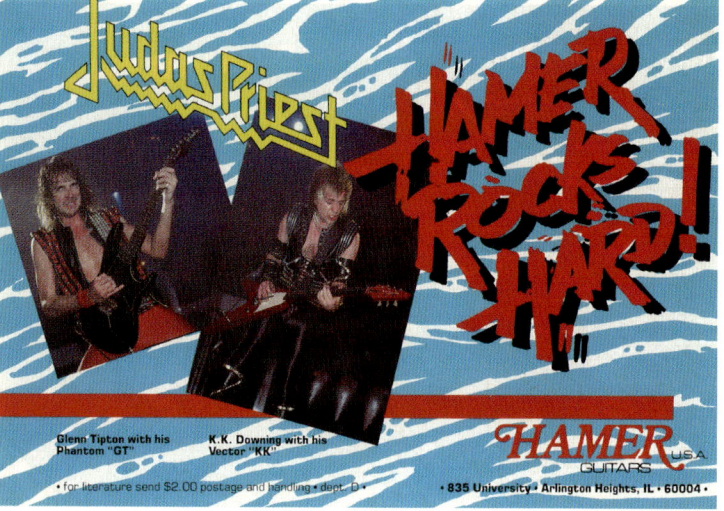

● This **1976 Hamer Standard** (main guitar) defined the new brand's outlook: a classic Gibson design reworked for a fresh breed of guitarists and their angular music. Hamer's '75 **catalogue** (right) emphasised the clean lines of the maple-top Standard, which continues to draw players such as No Doubt's **Tom Dumont**, pictured in this 1997 Hamer **ad** (below).

FLYING V ■ EXPLORER ■ FIREBIRD

HAMER'S NEW STANDARD

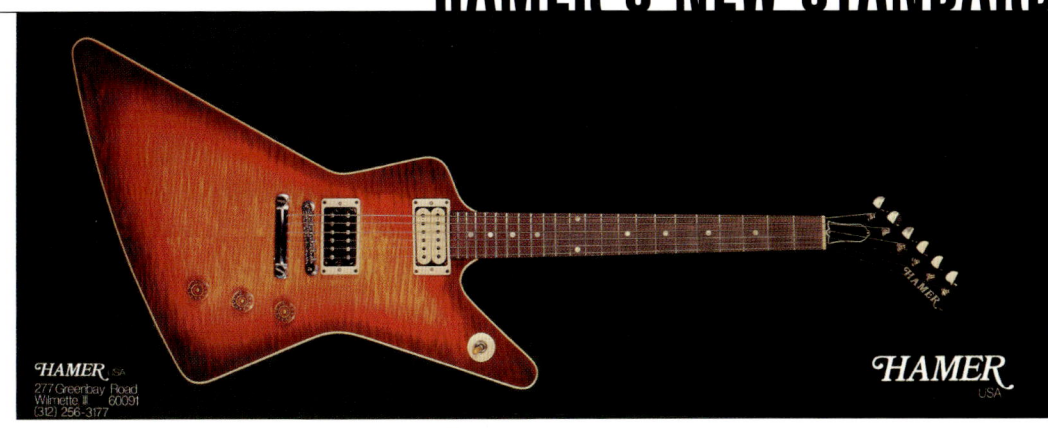

● Players were still discovering how good Gibson's '67-style Flying V could be, including **Mick Ralphs**, pictured (right) in the studio in London with Mott The Hoople in 1971. Ralphs often used mainstream guitars, but in Mott, and later with Bad Company, he would occasionally reach for something unusual. In the 70s and into the 80s, some players began to find that newer brands such as Hamer, Dean, B.C. Rich, and others had a better feel for the unusual. Judas Priest's **KK Downing**, for example, was featured on this 1985 Hamer **ad** (left) with a custom V-shaped axe.

FLYING V ■ EXPLORER ■ FIREBIRD

FLYING V ■ EXPLORER ■ FIREBIRD

NIELSEN: SHOWMAN & COLLECTOR

- **Rick Nielsen** of Cheap Trick is one of the best-known players to use Hamer guitars (1979 **ad**, opposite). He is also an avid collector, and may be the only individual to own two **Gibson Explorers** from the original 50s run of 22 examples: his two '58s are shown here (top and bottom). Nielsen proudly uses some of his valuable gems onstage: he's pictured with an original **Flying V** aloft at a Cheap Trick gig in 1979 (above) and also a few years earlier backstage with **Andy Warhol** (below), the artist clearly taken with this particular item of industrial art. Nielsen is noted for several spectacular guitars, not least a celebrated five-neck Hamer, but also this **1978 Hamer Checkerboard Standard** (main guitar), the finish developed in collaboration with 3M.

FLYING V ■ EXPLORER ■ FIREBIRD

Western brands. Gradually the guitars began to resemble particular models, if not always their precise construction.

In 1972, Hoshino became a partner in Harry Rosenblum's Elger Company, based in Ardmore, Pennsylvania, and Elger became the exclusive US distributor for Hoshino's products. Elger first showed Ibanez products at the June 1973 NAMM show in Chicago. A number of models also became available at this time in the UK through distributor Summerfield Brothers – some with Summerfield-specified brands such as CSL and Sumbro and others with Ibanez – and through J.T. Coppock with the Antoria brand.

The first Ibanez Flying V copy appeared in 1973. It was known in the USA as model 2387 Rocket Roll and was based on the '67-style triangular-control-layout V. The list price was $265, which made it $100 or so cheaper than the recently discontinued Gibson V. A couple of years later, the Ibanez 2387CT Rocket Roll Sr copied the original '58-style Flying V. A reverse Firebird lookalike, the 2348 Firebrand, came along in 1974, while an Explorer copy, the 2459 Destroyer, was first listed in '75 – Eddie Van Halen played a Destroyer during Van Halen's early days. Ibanez launched a Moderne copy, the 2469 Futura, in 1974. Remarkably, this Ibanez model was the first commercially-available instrument to interpret the Moderne design since Gibson's exploratory patent back in 1957.

It's hardly surprising that Gibson was irritated – and it wasn't just the copying that annoyed the executives in Kalamazoo. If the language Hoshino used in its promo material is anything to go by, the company had a shameless attitude. "This fall's new look in guitars is actually an old look," it said about the blatant copy of Gibson's '67-style Flying V. "The Ibanez Rocket Roll model features the look and sound of the guitar made famous by The Kinks, The Rolling Stones, Albert King, Savoy Brown, and many other well known performers."[57] An ad for the same model went further: "We don't have to tell you about the demand for oldies. Ibanez 'new oldies' are made to look like, play like, and sound like the models that inspired them. And just to show you that our nostalgia is in the right place, most Ibanez 'new oldies' sell for less than the 'old oldies' did when they were first introduced."[58]

Gibson did what most big companies do when angry: set loose the lawyers. And, again as with most big companies, this took a while. In 1977, Gibson's parent company, Norlin, finally took legal action against Ibanez's US arm, Elger. The action focussed on one area, with Norlin's lawyers alleging that Ibanez had copied and thus infringed the trademark of Gibson's distinctively-shaped three-tuners-a-side headstock, as used on Les Pauls and other models (but not on the V, Explorer, Firebird, or Moderne). Actually, Ibanez had by now moved to a different headstock shape anyway, but nonetheless there was a settlement out of court, with Elger promising not to copy Gibson. (Since the legal dispute, guitar collectors have indiscriminately used the term 'lawsuit' to describe more or less any oriental copy guitar of this period, regardless of whether or not it's an Ibanez.) Ibanez was forced to change direction away from blatant copies, but, ironically, it was the best thing that ever happened to them. The company's designers began to develop original models in the years following the dispute, and in fact some work of that kind had already begun, including the refined Artist double-cutaway shape and the dramatic Iceman design. The angular Iceman, which debuted in 1976, looked as if a Firebird had been given a curved and pointed base and a Rickenbacker-like hooked lower horn with a deeper cutaway. The following year, Paul Stanley of Kiss moved from a Gibson Flying V to an Ibanez Iceman, notably choosing to play a custom model with a spectacular broken-mirror finish – and suddenly everyone knew about this brave and distinctive development in pointy-guitar design.

A few years later, Ibanez issued a signature Paul Stanley Iceman model, the PS10. Stanley said that when he first went to see Ibanez in Japan he was impressed with how accommodating and how keen to learn the company was. "And they obviously have the facilities to make anything," he said in 1978. "That's a lot more than can be said for [the USA] at the moment. Japan really is the country of the future."[59] By the late 70s, Ibanez was more popular than ever, and the same was happening with other Japanese brands. Meanwhile, Gibson and most of the big US makers suffered as the oriental rise continued.

A few new US makers were stirring the pot, too, not least Bernardo Rico. As a young flamenco and classical guitarist, Rico enjoyed making acoustic guitars in his father's Los Angeles workshop in the early 60s. At the end of that decade he'd made his first electrics, but after setting up his own B.C. Rich firm he created some remarkably outlandish pointy designs that drew from and expanded upon the Explorer in particular.

Most notable of Rich's designs was the Mockingbird, launched in 1976, a curved and pointed modern interpretation of the Explorer shape, with onboard pre-amp and multiple switches, which found favour with Joe Perry and Slash, among others. Two years later, Rich offered the new Bich, with a scooped and sculpted body. Metal guitarists flocked to play Rich's devilish inventions, including Slayer's Kerry King, who still plays a Flying V derivative. Following Bernardo's death in 1999, B.C. Rich's new owners have continued to offer a full line of extreme pointy models, including those two originals as well as the Eagle, Warlock, Ironbird, and others.

Dean Zelinsky started the Dean guitar company in 1976 at the age of 19, and his first instruments went on sale the following year. They were the Dean V, the Dean Z, and the Dean ML (named for his best friend Matt Lynn, who died of cancer when they were 17). The first two were, respectively, like a Flying V and an Explorer, but as with Hamer had figured-wood tops, and the third had a new body design that simply and cleverly combined the two into a star-shaped concoction. They were the pointiest guitars yet, and by the early 80s they would be among the prime weapons for metal guitarists everywhere.

"You have to think back to where rock was in the late 70s," says Zelinsky. "For me, Woodstock in '69 was the beginning of modern-day rock, and from there it started to get a bit more sophisticated. But while the music was getting progressive, and on stage

● **Ibanez** was one of the first Japanese brands to copy classic US guitars. The 1975 **ad** (below) has knock-offs of the Explorer, Moderne, and Flying V, while this **1979 Rocket Roll II** (main guitar) is more of a Hamer-style V.

82

FLYING V ■ EXPLORER ■ FIREBIRD

IBANEZ: FROM COPIES TO ORIGINALS

Following the blatant copies of its formative years and a Gibson lawsuit, **Ibanez** began to create its own designs, including the Iceman. This **1979 Iceman IC-210** (right) reveals an odd meeting of Rickenbacker and Firebird in the body style. **Paul Stanley** of Kiss found the Iceman suited his on-stage flamboyance, and a series of **Iceman**-like signature models followed, not only from Ibanez but also Washburn. Stanley is pictured (below) in 1979 with a distinctive Iceman featuring a cracked-mirror finish. Ibanez would issue many more pointy creations, such as this extreme **1985 XV-500** (above)

FLYING V ■ EXPLORER ■ FIREBIRD

83

they're wearing cool clothes and have these great lightshows, to me it seemed funny that people were still playing un-flashy guitars designed in the 50s. I guess the carpet didn't match the cushions, you know? My whole concept was to bring along something sexy and stagey, where the guitar would become part of the look, and to put quality components on the guitar so that people would want to play it."

Zelinsky showed those first Dean models at the January 1977 NAMM 'Western Market' show at the Disneyland Convention Complex in Anaheim, California. He recalls the feeling that there was a new movement of guitar makers and suppliers at that time. "A lot of people – Seymour Duncan, DiMarzio, Wayne Charvel, B.C. Rich, Hamer – were showing for the first time at NAMM around then. It was a historical time in the music business: there was a surge in new pickups and parts and new guitar brands."

Why did it all happen at this particular time? "In every industry – motorcycles, cars, whatever – there's people who hot-rod," says Zelinsky. "Guitars was no different. I guess everybody saw it as an opportunity, mostly because Gibson and Fender were not on their game. If they had been on their game, I don't know that we would have been successful. Bottom line, for Gibson, I think it was management and ownership and corporations, and all the negativity that comes along with that. So, coincidentally, this group of new people all started at the same time."

Dean left that '77 NAMM show with over $40,000 worth of orders for his three models: the V, the Explorer-like Z, and the multi-point ML. All Zelinsky had to do now was build the guitars – which he and his small team of workers managed in the midst of the familiar problems that plague almost every small guitar firm. But once the Dean instruments were out there in the shops, he discovered that it's not just about offering good guitars. "I had two things going against me," Zelinsky says.

The first was that some people didn't like his headstock design: it was large and V-shaped, rather like the one on the original Futura/Explorer. "The other thing was brand. Guitar is all about brand. People are always worried what their friends are going to think when they show up with a new guitar. Specially an expensive guitar. Back then, my guitars were $100 more than a Les Paul – although a Les Paul was only $850. Brand was our enemy. We just didn't have it." Brand arrived for Dean in the shape of Kerry Livgren and a half-naked woman.

Zelinsky explains: "About the 13th Dean ever built I sold to Kerry Livgren of the band Kansas, and they just had that song 'Wayward Son' that was huge. They were off on tour to support it, and he was playing a Dean Z, the Explorer-shape one." Zelinsky ran an ad trumpeting the Kansas connection. "I think it gave me some instant credibility. A lot of guys will be in the guitar business for ten years and only hope to have a rock star play their guitars. I was in the business about ten minutes, and here was a rock star playing a Dean." Soon, top artists of the 80s, including ZZ Top, The Doobie Brothers, The Cars, Heart, Iron Maiden, Def Leppard, and Sammy Hagar, were playing Dean guitars.

THE SEVENTIES

Then there were Those Ads. If you were reading guitar magazines around 1980 you will remember the Dean ads. "There's this famous ad of a girl in a bikini standing in the water holding a V. To me it was a cool ad," says Zelinsky. "It was hot chicks, hot guitars, rock'n'roll, and all that. Nobody was doing that. All the other ads were like the craftsman on the bench turning the truss-rod and looking down with his bifocal glasses. I just wanted to say OK, we're your guy. We understand it. We get it. That was the concept of the ad. This girl had a mesmerising look, and it had a lot of impact."

The ads did what every business dreams its ads will do. They became controversial, and lots of guitar players were saying hey, have you seen that Dean ad? Today, we'd say it went viral. Readers regularly debated in the letters pages of *Guitar Player* magazine about whether these were sexist ads, or great ads, or something in between. "We were doing OK before that," smiles Zelinsky, "but that was a game-changer. All of a sudden, Dean became a household word, and as soon as that happened, guitars with the Dean brand started moving off the shelf quicker."

There was little doubt about the quality of the guitars, says Zelinsky, but once they had brand, everything changed. "And then one artist talks to another artist, networking backstage, and we pulled in a lot of artists pretty quick. In the 80s, I don't want to say we dominated MTV – this was when MTV was really about music and rock, which seems like light years ago – but in the original MTV video awards, there was a Dean guitar in the video-of-the-year for three of the first four years running."

A significant artist that Dean pulled in was Dimebag Darrell. Zelinsky first came across the young rocker in the early 80s, when a teenage Dimebag would regularly win the talent contests staged by a Dallas music store, Arnold & Morgan.

"I used to sponsor these contests, and he won a Dean ML," Zelinsky recalls. "He won other guitars, but he cut his teeth on this ML – and you could make a strong argument that Dimebag Darrell was one of the early pioneers of metal. So this probably cemented the ML as a metal-worthy guitar. The metal guys were looking to guitars to be more like rock'n'roll weapons. A Les Paul just doesn't look like a weapon." Zelinsky reports that Dimebag liked the way he could move with his ML – which through a circuitous route ended up refinished in blue with a lightning-bolt graphic – aside from the obvious requirements of sound and playability. "He used to fly around the stage, and it was a big guitar: he would have his arms out and keep the guitar in control, whereas a smaller guitar could get away from him. With the ML, he could keep his arms on the guitar but not look stupid."

Dimebag rose to success with his band Pantera. After they split in 2003, the guitarist was settling in with his new band, Damageplan, when he was shot dead on stage at a gig in Ohio at the end of 2004. Dimebag had been playing Washburn guitars since the mid 90s, but at the time of his shocking death he was working with Zelinsky on a new Dean model. Zelinsky, too, had been on a sabbatical away from Dean, having left in 1991. He came back in 2000, at first as a consultant, but soon he again became the major force in

● **Dean Zelinsky** started his **Dean** brand in 1976 – he's pictured a few years later (far right) with a slew of his pointy creations. His first trio of designs (1977 **ad**, above right) were based on the Gibson Flying V (the V) and Explorer (the Z), and a new third model (the ML) that merged the two. This **1977 ML** (main guitar) shows how he effectively matched the top and bottom halves of the older models to make his new design. Dean's marketing efforts were assisted when **Kerry Livgren** of Kansas (1977 **ad**, above centre) endorsed a Dean Z at the time his band had a big hit. Yet more impact came with a series of **ads** (1981 example, above left) that paired girls and guitars.

86　　　　　　　　　　　　　　　FLYING V ■ EXPLORER ■ FIREBIRD

DEAN'S FLYING EXPLORER

● **Dean** had learned the value of big-name endorsers from the experience with Kansas in the 70s, so it seemed a natural step in the 80s to publicise the fact that **Dimebag Darrell** (**ad**, above) was playing a Dean ML. Following a period when Dimebag switched to Washburn, he was working with Dean on a new design when he was shot dead at a gig in 2004. Another pioneer of pointy guitars was **Bernardo Rico** (right); this **1979 B.C. Rich Mockingbird** (centre) is typical of Rico's designs.

FLYING V ■ EXPLORER ■ FIREBIRD

87

● Although **Eric Clapton** is best known for his work with Strats and Les Pauls, he's tried other guitars, like the Explorer pictured earlier (see p31). He used another **1958 Explorer** (below) in the 70s – seen (left) on a 1974 date in Holland. Clapton cut off part of the body, near where his right arm fell, to make it more comfortable. He sold it later in the 70s and today it's owned by a collector.

90 FLYING V ■ EXPLORER ■ FIREBIRD

OLD EXPLORER DISCOVERS A NEW V

● **Gibson** had let the Flying V go out of production in the early 70s, but with all the new interest in pointy guitars the company reissued the '67-style design in 1975. This **ad** from that same year (above right) was part of the publicity campaign to remind players how much demand there was for the originals. This **1979 Flying V** (above) shows the revised model, while a 1977 **ad** (right) offers a T-shirt decal with **Firebird 76** logo. More players were trying the Ibanez copies of classic Gibsons, including **Sylvain Sylvain** (top) of The New York Dolls with his Flying V.

FLYING V ■ EXPLORER ■ FIREBIRD

different approach. "We were looking for something that hadn't been done before, and Chuck Burge devised a shape that was graceful: kind of a mellowed-out, more rounded Explorer. We enlisted the synthesizer designer Bob Moog to come up with an active circuit – we had never done active guitars prior to that time – and he came up with the RD's new expansion and compression features."

Active circuitry was popularized by electric-bass specialist Alembic at the start of the 70s, designed to boost the signal and widen the tonal range of an electric guitar. This kind of hi-fidelity approach was prompted by the apparent competition from synthesizers, which had become big business during the late 70s. Gibson's parent company Norlin figured that a hook-up with Moog, one of the synthesizer field's most famous names, might re-capture ground that guitars seemed to be losing to the new keyboards.

"I remember going out to Bob Moog's place in the middle of February," says Bolen. "There was three feet of snow, and we went into his barn, which was his studio and scientific lab. He took us through a bunch of different things, trying sounds. I liked what he did – it was a guitar that could give you that harmonic pinch thing very easily, and a lot of guys were just starting to get into that. And with the expansion circuit, well … you had enough highs there to slice cheese."[62]

One of the RD models, the Standard, was a regular electric, without the active circuit, which was reserved for the Custom and Artist models. But the line did not prove popular, and many guitarists disliked what they considered the 'unnatural' sounds of active circuitry, a major factor in the downfall of the series. Gibson believed the radical styling was more to blame, and a little later put the RD technology into the traditional body designs of an ES thinline and a Les Paul solidbody. These, too, failed to grab players and did not last. The various RD models were gone from the catalogue by 1981.

Elsewhere, Randy Rhoads hit the big time in 1979 when he left his own band, Quiet Riot, to join Ozzy Osbourne. By then, the guitarist was playing mainly a white Les Paul and a Sandoval Flying V finished in black with white polka-dots. Custom maker Karl Sandoval had built the V that year, to Rhoads's plan, deploying a Mighty Mite V body, a modified old Danelectro neck, bow-tie fingerboard inlays, a Strat-style jack in the crotch of the V, and a layout of Fender vibrato, two DiMarzio humbuckers, and four controls. Rhoads made his first album with Ozzy, *Blizzard Of Ozz*, and when the record was released in 1980 it was immediately obvious what a talent he was. Rhoads decided to have a new V-style guitar made, and he went to see Grover Jackson.

We met Jackson earlier, as a young guitarist in his native Tennessee with an eye for unusual instruments. He moved to California and in 1978 bought what he describes as a "bankrupt little repair shop"– the start of Charvel Jackson. He was aware of Randy Rhoads as a noteworthy young guitarist around Los Angeles who'd suddenly found fame by joining Ozzy's band. Just before Christmas 1980, Jackson's phone rang. It was Randy, who said he needed to get a guitar made. "He'd come home from Ozzy in Europe, for

Christmas," says Jackson. "I said OK, cool. But he called I think on December 22, and of course I'd already turned everybody loose for the holidays."

Rhoads popped over to Jackson's shop the next day and stayed until midnight, the pair talking over music, guitars, and whatnot. "He took out this little cocktail napkin," Jackson recalls, "with a kind of line drawing on it, like four or five angular lines. And that was his contribution. It was his idea to do the pointy thing. I added on the head as we scribbled and scratched around. That's how the Rhoads guitar was born."

Rhoads took delivery of his new Jackson around March 1981. Its pointy offset-V body was finished in white with black pinstripe detailing, and it had a vibrato bridge/tailpiece, two humbuckers and four controls, a block-inlay board, and Jackson's take on the droopy Explorer-style headstock. Rhoads immediately put it to good use, especially on tour dates. Even then, however, he began to hunger for a more extreme design. "Randy said that people were coming up to him at shows and asking if this was a Flying V that'd been butchered," recalls Jackson. "He said he wanted it more sharkfin-like."

By now, the Charvel Jackson shop was finding its feet. "We were learning the craft," Jackson explains. "It was on-the-job training. Manufacturing was really modest at the time," he says, and laughs at his own spin. "What I really mean is that we didn't know what the fuck we were doing, basically. But because I knew what a good guitar was supposed to play like and feel like, from my experience with the vintage stuff, at least when we got close I could say, well, it needs to be more this or more that. It wasn't that I knew how to do it, it was that I knew where I wanted to go. And we had the tenacity at the time to stick with it until we got it."

In his time, Jackson has seen everything from the player who wants to know the size of every screw in his guitar to the one who wishes merely to have a good guitar, and to hell with the details. "Some guys take the hot-rod approach, and some guys take the musical approach. And Randy was the musical approach. It was my experience that he wouldn't even play a new guitar when he first got it. He would just open the case and look at it, then close the case; the next day he'd open it and look at it, then close the case; then maybe a week or so later he'd pick it up and play a few notes and then put it away. He had to kind of warm up to it."

Rhoads came over and they worked on the new design. They'd lay down the original template, trace around that; Rhoads would suggest a little more here, a little less there. "Then we'd erase it or sand it off, and then redraw it," says Jackson. "Finally, there was the point where he said yeah, that's it, let's do that. I said OK, let me take it over to the bandsaw and hack it out. And he said oh, I can't watch that. He went in the office. I went and hacked it out, and then I took it into the office and said: is this about what you're talking about? He said yeah, that's great. And that's how the current design was done."[63]

Rhoads commissioned three Jacksons with the new design, only the first of which, finished in black, was completed for him. The immediately distinctive feature of the new

● **Grover Jackson** began his guitar firm in the late 70s in California and became known for the superstrat, but he also indulged players who wanted outlandish designs. One such was **Randy Rhoads**, whose first Jackson V (he's pictured with it, far right) led to a design with an extreme pointy 'wing', seen in this **1983 Randy Rhoads** (below), which is still made today as the RR. There was also a twin-wing design, seen in this **1984 Double Rhoads Custom** (right).

FLYING V ■ EXPLORER ■ FIREBIRD

FROM RD TO RHOADS

- Gibson's **RD series** (1979 ad, right) was a brave attempt to match Moog synth circuitry to the electric guitar. As this **1979 RD Artist** shows (above), the RDs had a sort of curvy Firebird look, and the multiple controls offered active tone as well as compression and expansion. Players largely ignored the potential of these techno-axes, and they were gone from the line by 1981.

- **Randy Rhoads** (right) was best known for the recordings he made with Ozzy Osbourne. Rhoads's career was cut short by a light-aircraft accident in 1982 when he was just 26. He loved V-shaped guitars, and the custom model he's pictured with was one of four guitars that Grover **Jackson** made for him.

FLYING V ■ EXPLORER ■ FIREBIRD

95

● **Grover Jackson** (right) and his Jackson brand were the most important 80s innovators, using pointy bodies, extreme vibratos, and a superstrat vibe. Jackson headed his firm until 1989, when corporate pressure became too much. The brand continues, and many pointy creations have appeared through the years, including this **1990 Warrior** (below).

FLYING V ■ EXPLORER ■ FIREBIRD

WARRIOR, WYLDE, & BOOMERANG

● This **1981 Gibson V2** (main guitar) came out in 1979 as a partner to the equally unusual Explorer E/2 (1980 **ad**, below). Both featured highly sculpted multi-laminate bodies, and the V2 had remarkable Boomerang V-shaped pickups. Both had disappeared by 1982.

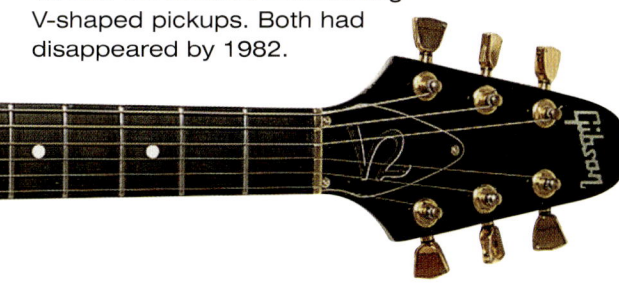

● A gathering of **Charvel Jackson** players for this 1985 **ad** (right) includes pointys and superstrats with players such as Steve Vai, Jake E. Lee, and Steve Lynch. **Zakk Wylde** played a Jackson V early in his career, and also this polka-dot V (top right) made by GMW Guitarworks to match a guitar used by Randy Rhoads. Today, Wylde plays mainly Gibson Les Pauls.

FLYING V ■ EXPLORER ■ FIREBIRD

the Flying V, however, the R&D staff failed to track down an original to use as their model. Instead, remarkably, they used a large picture of a 50s V featured on a poster issued by a German vintage dealer, Music No.1 of Hamburg. "Chuck Burge redrew the body drawings off of that poster, and so we ended up with some proportioning errors. We also decided not to have the body overlap the neck joint," says Shaw. "Later on, we got flagged in the trade press because the guitar was not exactly accurate. We did find the correct floor-mat material for the traction-strip on the body edge, however, and the Gibson logo on the headstock was from the original tooling. We made an effort, but some things worked better than others – and not being able to get an original does rather handicap you."[68]

Then it was time to do the Moderne. This, you'll remember, was the name invented later for the design included with the Flying V and Explorer in the original trio of patents that Gibson applied for in 1957. As we've seen, it's unlikely that Gibson got any further than the patent. So here was Gibson in the early 80s about to 'reissue' a guitar that had never appeared in the first place. (An earlier development in this bizarre story had come in 1974 when the Japanese maker Ibanez produced a 'copy' of this non-existent guitar, calling the result the Futura.)

R&D boss Bruce Bolen thought it would be fun for Gibson to produce a Moderne. "Collectors were starting up then," he recalls, "and these guys were looking for all kinds of weird stuff. So I thought, well, I can't think of anything weirder than a Moderne."[69] Of course, no original existed, so Gibson had to use the only piece of information they had: the 50s patent. Tim Shaw had a friend whose girlfriend's dad was an architect, and in the architect's office was a specialist large-scale Xerox copier. "We knew the size of the nut-to-12th-fret scale, and we knew how wide a pickup was," says Shaw. "So I gave my friend the patent drawing and told him to sneak into this architect's office and pop this thing up until it's twelve-and-five-eighths from the nut to the centre of the 12th fret, and until the pickup is so big. Which he did. And that's why, in fact, the 80s Moderne is the way that it is."[70]

One modification they had to make to the dimensions of the patent drawing concerned the headstock. If they had followed the proportions of the patent, Shaw explains, the head would have been ridiculously large, around seven-and-a-half-inches wide. The head is hardly the most attractive feature of the ugly Moderne anyway – "I used to call it Gumby," says Bolen, recalling with some justification the US cartoon series that starred a stubby-headed character – and Shaw's decision was a good one.

"Our draughtsman Dale Campbell and I made an editorial decision to shrink the peghead proportionally," says Shaw. "And I made the editorial decision to wire it so that the pickguard fit more like an Explorer than a V. A Flying V is a very difficult instrument to assemble in production, because you're turning it over a lot: there's stuff that top-loads, stuff that back-loads, the strings go through the body, and there's that stupid jack out in the middle of nowhere. It's not an easy guitar to put together. Every time you have to turn a guitar over in production, it's a pain in the butt. I had a sense as an engineer that rational men looked at the V and said dear god, let's not ever do anything that stupid again. So I applied the same logic to the Moderne."[71]

Having dealt with the Heritage reissues, Gibson found time to come up with a new design even uglier than the Moderne, known as the Corvus or Futura (yes, that name again). Bolen points out that, in contrast, there were plenty of successes from the R&D team at the time – the Chet Atkins solidbody classical, B.B. King's Custom/Lucille, the Howard Roberts Fusion, and others. But the original inspiration for the Corvus/Futura came from the recent popularity of headless guitars. Steinberger started the trend with a headless electric bass in 1981, and within a short time almost every maker seemed keen to lop off the headstock and offer a headless guitar or two. Gibson was no exception.

Chuck Burge in R&D provided a design with a deep notch in the body base where the tuners, absent from the missing head, would reside. Bruce Bolen's R&D department was still based at the old buildings in Kalamazoo, but Gibson's marketing team was now located 500 miles away at the new factory in Nashville. "Marketing saw our prototype," recalls Bolen with a sigh, "and they went oh no, we've got to have a head on it. So they put what we called the limp-dick head on it – and totally screwed up the design." Gibson launched the new headstock-equipped production version in 1982 as the Futura, with through-neck construction, and the Corvus, with bolt-on neck, and each retained the peculiar body that looked a little like a misguided can-opener. These guitars went largely unpurchased and were gone from the catalogue within a couple of years.

Norlin decided to sell Gibson around this time. Sales had fallen by 30 percent in 1982 alone, to a total of $19.5 million, against a high in 1979 of $35.5 million. Gibson was not alone in this decline: the guitar market in general had virtually imploded, and most other American makers were suffering in broadly similar ways. Costs were high, economic circumstances and currency fluctuations were against them, and Japanese competitors increasingly had the edge.

Rooney Pace made a hostile takeover of Norlin in 1984, and chairman Norton Stevens was off the board. Norlin had relocated some of its administration staff from Chicago to Nashville around 1980, and all the main Gibson production was now handled at the Nashville plant. Kalamazoo had become a specialist factory making custom orders, banjos, and mandolins, and as far as Norlin was concerned the closure of this factory was inevitable. Kalamazoo produced its last instruments in June 1984, and the plant closed three months later, after more than 65 years of worthy service since Gibson erected the original building. It was an emotional time for managers and workers, many of whom had worked in the plant for a considerable time. Three of them – Jim Deurloo, Marv Lamb, and J.P. Moats – rented part of the Kalamazoo plant and started the new Heritage guitar company in April 1985. Over at the Nashville plant, the

● **Pete Townshend** (right) dug deep into his collection to feature an original-style Flying V for the jacket of his 1982 album *All The Best Cowboys Have Chinese Eyes*.

FLYING V ■ EXPLORER ■ FIREBIRD

MODERNISTIC MODERNE

● This **1983 Corvus** (left) came from Gibson's attempt to make a headless guitar: the tuners were intended to sit in the 'notch' in the guitar body. The sales team demanded a conventional head; the result was the Corvus (bolt-neck) or Futura (set neck; 1983 **catalogue**, below). The US-map-shape guitar on a 1983 **ad** (below left) looks almost tasteful by comparison.

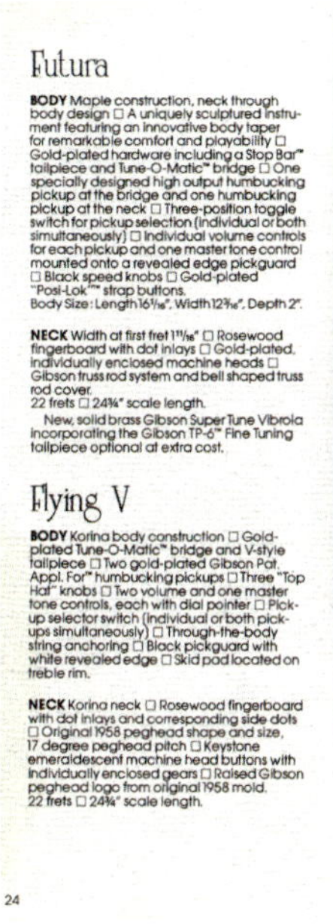

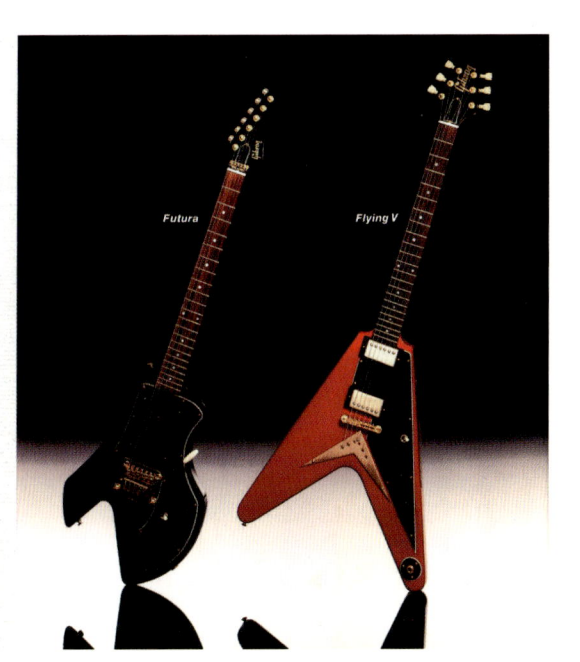

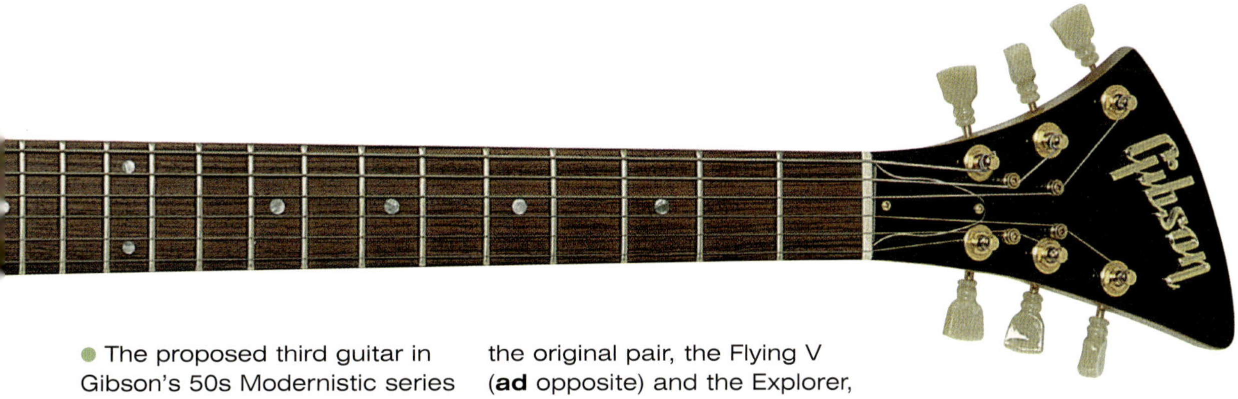

● The proposed third guitar in Gibson's 50s Modernistic series probably never got further than a patent drawing (see p30), and among collectors the design later became known as the **Moderne**. In the early 80s, Gibson produced reissues of the original pair, the Flying V (**ad** opposite) and the Explorer, but it also took the opportunity to produce a 'reissue' ... of the guitar that never existed. This **1982 Moderne** (main guitar) shows how Gibson interpreted the original 50s patent.

FLYING V ■ EXPLORER ■ FIREBIRD

103

emphasis had been on large runs of a small number of models, but this had to change when it became Gibson's sole factory.

Norlin had put Gibson up for sale around 1980, and by summer 1985 they finally found a buyer. In January 1986, Henry Juszkiewicz, David Berryman, and Gary Zebrowski, three businessmen who had met while classmates at Harvard business school, completed their purchase of Gibson for $5 million. The inevitable 'restructuring' of the business occurred, and as usual this meant that many employees lost their jobs.

As for the Explorer and Flying V, Gibson did little to further the idea of accurate original reissues following its well-meaning attempt with the early-80s Heritage models, and instead put out a number of revised and modified designs, usually following various trends of the time. The two principal 80s versions were skewed modern takes: in 1984, Gibson introduced an Explorer that had no pickguard and featured its three knobs in a triangular layout, and in the same year released a Flying V, also pickguard-less, and with the controls in a curving line. They lasted as Gibson's primary Explorer and V models to the end of the decade.

Experiments of the moment included the 1984 Designer series with fashionable custom graphics for Explorer and V, an Explorer Synthesizer model the following year with extra Roland 700 synth pickup and controls, various XPL instruments that adopted super-pointy shapes, and multiple pickup combinations on models such as the Explorer 400 and the Flying V Double. Gibson stayed very quiet with the Firebird through the 80s, probably not helped when its contemporary attempt at a Fender-like design, the Victory models of 1981, was not successful. The Victorys had disappeared from the line within three years.

One of the biggest boosts in the 80s for the popularity of pointy guitars came when Edge of U2 played a 1976 Explorer on almost all the band's early records and live shows, and it's remained one of his favourite instruments ever since. The teenage Edge bought the instrument in or around the year it was made, while on holiday in New York City with his parents. "At that stage I didn't know very much about guitars, and I didn't really have a clue what I wanted," he said, "although I had a pretty good idea of what I didn't want. I just went into a shop and started to try things out. Rickenbackers sounded a bit limited, and I wasn't overly impressed with the Les Pauls I played. Then I picked up the Explorer, with its strange shape, and there seemed to be so much more variety in the sounds I could get from it."

Edge found the Explorer's neck pickup pleasantly mellow and the bridge pickup usefully powerful but with an appealing clarity. "It had none of that rasping, growling distortion you get from a Les Paul," he said in 1982. "The top strings sounded richer, too, where the Les Pauls were all on the thin side. I could play little chords on the top three strings and they'd feel really full. My style is based on a lot of broken chords and picking, and the Explorer seems to be quite the perfect guitar for it."

When U2 recorded their first album, *Boy*, in Dublin in 1980, their producer Steve Lillywhite was surprised to find such a lean set-up confronting him from the other side of the glass. Edge recalled: "He was astonished at how little gear U2 had as a band: one guitar, one bass, a drum kit, and a couple of amps was about the extent of it. But the Explorer was the only guitar I owned for quite a long time."[72]

More than any other band, it was Metallica who carved the modern metal template, and during the 80s the band laboured hard to build their success, defining a genre with *Master Of Puppets* in 1986 and celebrating their first US Number One album, *Metallica*, five years later. Guitarists Kirk Hammett and James Hetfield worked their way through an arsenal of largely pointy guitars: Hammett started with Gibson Vs and a Jackson Rhoads, while Hetfield favoured Gibson Explorers at first. Both moved to ESP guitars toward the end of the 80s and have more or less stuck to them ever since, and while both settled on relatively conventionally-styled signature models, the 2011 Snakebyte models for Hetfield introduced an intriguing new Explorer-influenced shape.

ESP, or Electric Sound Products, began as a small custom shop in the back of a Tokyo music store in 1975, established by Hisatake Shibuya, who gradually expanded his business to include manufacturing, retail, and music education. At first, Shibuya's guitars were copies, but especially when he opened his first overseas office, in New York City in 1985, the potential for original takes on traditional models became clearer. Matt Masciandaro, currently president and CEO of ESP, joined in 1987. "At that time," he says, "we were making reproductions of vintage instruments and just beginning to experiment with our own designs. In addition, we were selling replacement parts for electric guitars, and everything was built at our own factory in Japan."

ESP's main business continued in copies and superstrats, but there were custom-shop specials and signature models, too, including pointy designs, as well as production models such as the mid-90s signature V for Kerry King and the V/NV and EX series, since 1999 featuring extreme V and extended Explorer-style shapes. "We gradually shifted the focus toward ESP designs and custom instruments," says Masciandaro. "We earned a reputation as the company offering an alternative to 'your father's guitar', with the ability to build instruments with graphics, custom inlays, unique shapes, and so on. This attracted a lot of players and endorsers, many of whom we still work with, including Kirk Hammett and James Hetfield of Metallica, George Lynch, Ron Wood, and Slayer."[73] ESP added a second-tier budget-level brand, LTD, in 1996.

Gibson certainly noticed the popularity of ESP's pointy models, and in the late 90s took legal action, resulting in a settlement in 1999 in a Nashville court. "As a result of this action regarding Explorer and Flying V shapes that both companies were using at the time," says Masciandaro, "ESP agreed to use modified versions of each shape, which we introduced in 1999, and these are the EX and V shapes we still use today."[74] The two companies agreed that ESP would not use "the shape and appearance of any of Gibson's

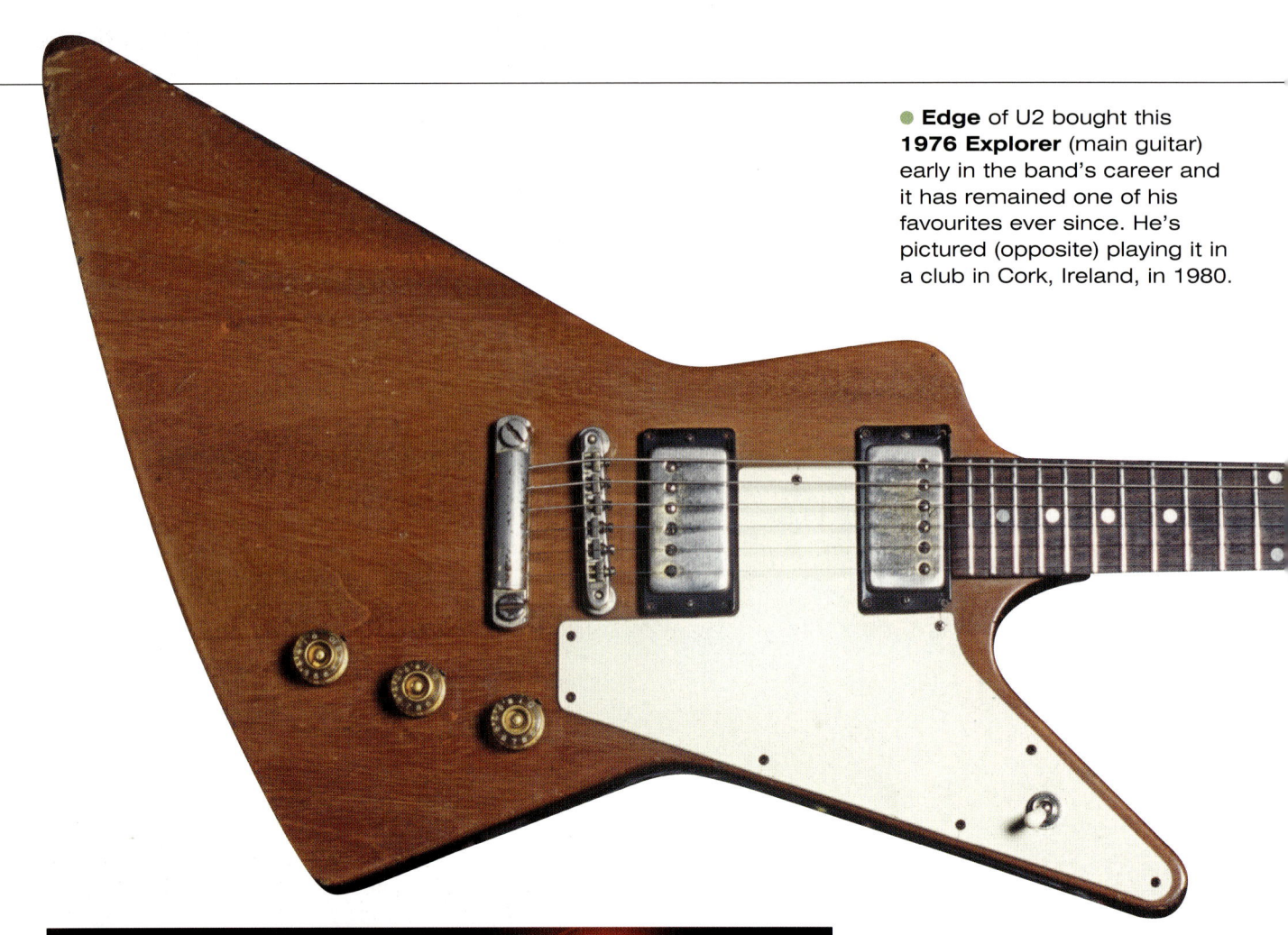

● **Edge** of U2 bought this **1976 Explorer** (main guitar) early in the band's career and it has remained one of his favourites ever since. He's pictured (opposite) playing it in a club in Cork, Ireland, in 1980.

● **Metallica** have set the bar for much of modern metal's scope and flavour, and that includes the genre's predilection for pointy guitars. **James Hetfield** (left) has almost always favoured Explorer-style axes, and he's pictured here on-stage in Los Angeles in 1988 with a custom guitar built by the Japanese maker ESP. **Gibson**, meanwhile, came up with some garish finishes (1984 **ad**, right) for the Flying V and Explorer in an attempt to seduce metal players, bringing together the shortlived "special look" as the **Designer Series**.

FLYING V ■ EXPLORER ■ FIREBIRD

U2 CAN BE AN EXPLORER

● We've seen that many makers – including Hamer, Dean, Jackson, B.C. Rich, and others – have been influenced by Gibson's original Flying V, Explorer, and Firebird designs over the years. But arch-rivals Fender largely ignored the trend ... until the mid 80s. This **1985 Katana** (above) is like a V without legs. It did not last long.

Express yourself... with Gibson.

The Gibson Designer Series

Now you can order a unique, custom designed finish on your new Gibson Explorer or Flying V for that special look on stage to go with your special sound.

Whether you choose a Custom Graphic design or a one-of-a-kind Artist Original, you'll have a superb, hand rubbed Gibson finish to assure lasting value.

See your nearest Gibson dealer for the full story. You'll like the price.

Gibson. Making history. Yesterday, Today, Tomorrow.

FLYING V ■ EXPLORER ■ FIREBIRD

107

● Then and now: Gibson used this shot of **Ted McCarty** (above), company boss in the 50s when the V and Explorer were designed, to promote 90s reissues; this **ESP Amakusa** (main guitar), built for a trade show in 2010, is about as pointy as a modern guitar can be.

110   FLYING V ■ EXPLORER ■ FIREBIRD

POINTY COMES FULL CIRCLE

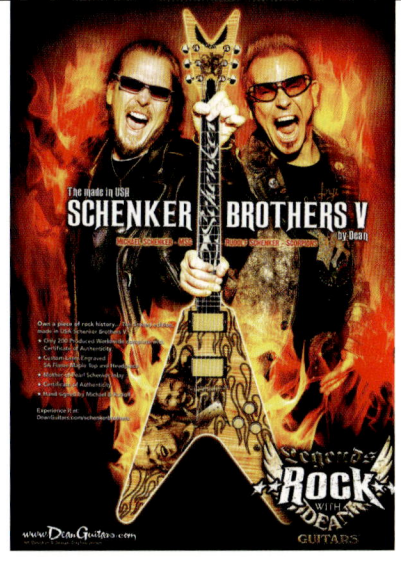

● The pointy guitar, invented by Gibson in the 50s, has today found its natural home in classic rock and metal. The aggressive look of an angular shape, complete with wings and star-like spikes, seems to perfectly match the ferocious roar of a full-on modern metal band. Players like **Alexi Laiho** of Children Of Bodom (with Rhoads-like ESP, 2007 **ad**, opposite) or **Gus G.** (with his signature ESP, on-stage with Ozzy in New York City in 2010, above) wouldn't look right with a more conventional guitar. Gibson certainly couldn't have foreseen back in the 50s what their Flying V and Explorer designs, commercial flops at the time, would lead to now. This book has shown how other makers – such as Dean (2006 Schenker V **ad**, top) – have drawn on and developed those prophetic originals. But as Ibanez points out in this recent **ad** (above) for its extreme-Explorer Xiphos: "It's only a guitar." Or is it?

FLYING V ■ EXPLORER ■ FIREBIRD

impressive line of archtop acoustics and electrics. "The space-age influenced consumer design in the late 50s, and Gibson answered with the 'modernistic' Korina Flying V and Explorer," ran the sales-pitch in Gibson's sumptuous Historic Collection brochure of 1994. "These guitars are the most highly sought of any Gibson solidbody. Precisely measured from samples of original 1958 instruments, the Historic Collection's Flying V and Explorer offer the modern collector a chance to own these rare pieces." Gibson even included in the brochure a picture of the ageing Ted McCarty alongside the two sprightly reissues. McCarty, you will recall, was the boss of Gibson back when the original V and Explorer appeared.

By coincidence, I spoke to the 83-year-old McCarty a few days after that photo session. McCarty, who had run his own Bigsby company since leaving Gibson way back in 1966, said: "They tell me that they're going to bring the Flying V back exactly like the originals. They're getting smart down there at Gibson – they want to have some of the old heritage guitars. They were here with their photographer for five or six hours, taking pictures of the Flying V and the other things: pictures of me holding them, pictures of me looking up as if someone just came in, pictures of me holding these various patents – that kind of thing."[79] The old boss did not seem overly impressed by the arrival of the new reissues.

Gibson's 'new' korina pair stayed in the catalogue more or less continually from that appearance in the early 90s until today, forming the backbone of the traditional Flying V and Explorer line for many years. At last, the modernistics were back where they belonged, and the circle appeared to be unbroken.

Also in the early 90s, the triangular-knobs large-pickguard V reappeared, surviving for ten years and more as the Flying V '67. And for the first time, Gibson issued a handful of shortlived signature Vs: a Jimi Hendrix '69 Custom in 1991, and then two years later Vs for Rudolf Schenker, Scorpions (effectively a Michael Schenker V), and Lonnie Mack (complete with Bigsby mounted in that awkward fashion in the space between the wings, just like Lonnie's original).

In the early 90s and again around 2000, the reverse Firebirds got the proper reissue treatment, with a I, III, V, and VII, the last three of which have survived through to the current line. And in general, Gibson has continued to tip its hat to key players and their loyalty by producing signature models, including an Allen Collins Explorer (2003), Lenny Kravitz Flying V (2001), and Johnny Winter Firebird (2008).

In recent years, Gibson has provided at least a core of historically accurate reissues of the Flying V, the Explorer, and the Firebird. It supplements these with a shifting mix of models that are influenced by the shapes and designs of the original models, but which are intended to reflect current tastes – sometimes rationally, other times apparently haphazardly – and offer modern appointments, finishes, and electronics. At the time of writing, that core consisted of a 60s-style Flying V and a '76-style Explorer (in other words the two mahogany-body versions), plus those three Firebirds (III, V, and VII). Gibson's second-tier brand, Epiphone, as ever added some cheaper models.

An interesting guitar for those of you who were taking notes in the earlier pages of this book was the Mahogany Futura, issued in 2002. For this, Gibson went back to the original patent for what became the Explorer, using the specific body design from that document, with its narrower waist compared with an Explorer and a striking V-shape headstock. There had been an earlier take on the idea, in 1996, but both were limited editions designed to excite collectors. Another idea aimed at lovers of old instruments is the aged guitar, which Fender popularised with its Relics, begun in the mid 90s. Gibson successfully employed the look, starting with its Les Paul Standard 59 Aged model in 1999, and applied it to the Worn Mahogany finish of the Epiphone Worn Firebird Studio (2007) and the Worn Cherry finish of the Gibson Flying V Faded model (2009).

Onboard electronics is one area where Gibson has obstinately refused to give up. In 2006, the company began shipping its long-promised digital guitar, the HD.6X-Pro, a Les Paul with extra hex pickup that allowed the player to feed various combinations of strings to a computer, for use with recording software. The next tech step came a year later with a series of Robot guitars. Various regular Gibsons – mainly Les Paul and SG models, but also an Explorer and Flying V launched in 2008 – were offered with the clever Robot self-tuning system, which uses powered pegs and provides standard tuning plus six programmable tunings. A further development came in 2010 with the peculiar Firebird X, an ugly take on a non-reverse Firebird with Robot tuning and onboard kitchen sink.

Players who've embraced pointiness in recent years include Tim Wheeler of Ash, who occasionally took a turn on a Flying V; Dave Grohl, seen with an Explorer in Foo Fighters and evidently also keen on Firebirds; Lenny Kravitz, who used a V among a variety of other axes; Gem Archer of Oasis, not averse to a non-reverse Firebird; Warren Haynes, primarily a Les Paul man but willing to try a side dish of Firebird; and Joe Bonamassa, another Les Paul aficionado, who in 2010 was happily strapping on a Flying V to play at the end of his live sets.

However, with those and a few other honourable exceptions aside, the pointy electric guitar has become largely the domain of metal musicians, who have the benefit of a large number of brands offering extreme-pointy models to choose from. Just to name a few examples among the possibilities, there's Dean and its sharkfin Razorback, Hamer with the relatively traditional Vector Korina, B.C. Rich and its gothic Beast, Jackson and the now-standard Rhoads design, ESP with the extended-V lines of the SV-II – and, of course, Gibson with something like the Explorer Vampire Blood Moon.

Let's see how a couple of modern metal men came to play their chosen weapons. Alexi 'Wildchild' Laiho is the singer and lead guitarist with Finland's Children Of Bodom, whose debut record appeared in 1997. Their 2008 album *Blooddrunk* was an especially well-crafted concoction, and Laiho has gained increasing attention among his fellow metal-fretters, not least for a knack for melodic invention over speedy riffing. He started on a Strat, but soon he wanted something more appropriate to a rising star of metal. "I liked the V-shaped guitars," he says, "but I didn't have one till like '97. I just tried one of them for the hell of it, a custom-made Jackson, and I fell in love with it."

What made him go for that V-style Jackson Rhoads? "I knew the guys from a band called Stone, and one of them played those kinds of guitars, and there was Anthrax, and some of the W.A.S.P. guys, like Chris Holmes." When his two custom Jackson Rhoads models were stolen, Laiho welcomed an approach in 2003 from ESP. "They stepped up and said they could make me guitars," he recalls. "I was kind of reluctant to switch brands at that time, but when I first tried ESP guitars I was totally in love with them." A signature model followed a couple of years later, interpreting the Rhoads theme, and one version even offered luminous coloured pinstripes. "So many people said oh dude, that pink pinstripe guitar is like the gayest guitar I've ever seen – but then those same guys really wanted to have one. So yeah, that's one of my favourites," he laughs.

He's uncertain why it is that so many metal players are drawn to pointy guitars. "I don't know … they just look mean," Laiho suggests. "They have an aggressive look, I guess, that fits metal real good."[80]

Gus G. replaced Zakk Wylde in Ozzy Osbourne's band in 2009 and still runs his own band, Firewind. Greek-born Gus, whose real name is Kostas Karamitroudis, also started with a Strat, but he'd noticed the Schenker brothers playing Vs and he knew very well that Hendrix had played one, too. "I thought, that's a cool guitar if I ever got something different, you know? When I started playing with this band Dream Evil, in Sweden, my first endorsement came in, with Washburn. They gave me one of the Dimebag guitars – but it was one of the unpopular ones, a Culprit."

For a few years, Gus played this pointy Explorer-style guitar, with its unusual hook in the body base ("we called it the beer-bottle opener"). But he was confused about the future of the relationship with Washburn. So when, during a promo visit to Japan, he was approached by representatives from the evidently resourceful ESP company, he listened carefully. "They were like: if you need any guitars, whatever you need, we'll make it for you." ESP figured that Gus was already known for the Culprit shape and suggested he play their similar Random Star – perhaps the best and most explicit model name ever conceived for an extreme-Explorer shape. "I really liked this one immediately," Gus says, "because I'm not a big tall guy, and that is a smaller guitar – it's like a smaller Dimebag, and not as pointy; more rounded."

By the time Gus joined Ozzy in 2009, he had his signature version, the ESP Gus G NT model. He relates the story of his arrival, pointy NT in hand, in the midst of the Ozzy clan. "Ozzy looked at this guitar, and he says: do you play Les Pauls? And I'm like, I hate Les Pauls. So he says, can you play a few songs with a Les Paul-shape guitar? Because, obviously, there is a history with Ozzy and his guitar players using Les Pauls." As the new boy stepping into Wylde's shoes, Gus was keen to compromise. "I'm thinking the Les Paul idea is a cool thing, I should do something like that. So that's how I developed my other signature model, the GUS-600. But I've got so used to playing with the NT shape that if I pick up any other guitar it feels strange now."

It's not just Ozzy who could have changed the course of Gus's pointy-guitar history. Gus himself almost took a different route when he was trying to find an alternative to his Washburn Culprit. "At that point, I was so disappointed with Washburn, I said if somebody doesn't make me a guitar that I like, right now, I'm just not going to bother. I'll just go out and buy a Gibson Flying V. That's what I would have done if ESP hadn't come along."

But isn't the Flying V an old-fashioned guitar? It's a guitar that was designed more than 20 years before Gus was even born. "Yeah," he laughs, "but that's what I had in mind. It is an old-fashioned guitar, but it never goes out of fashion. Everybody still plays it, really. It still looks current, I guess."[81]

The Flying V still looks current, and it never goes out of fashion. The Explorer isn't far behind, and you don't have to look much beyond to detect the influence of the Firebird. The V and Explorer in particular have had an enormous effect on other designers and guitar-makers, inspiring ever more jagged and sharkfin-like creations that find especially welcoming homes among metal musicians. Or, as Gibson said in its original publicity for the Flying V back in the 50s: "The swept-back, tapered lines of this really forward-looking instrument will be a real asset to the combo musician with a flair for showmanship."

It's still hard to imagine what prompted Gibson to come up with the Flying V and the Explorer originally. They were unlike anything that had gone before. "Every once in a while you try to stretch out of the box," says Bruce Bolen, R&D boss at Gibson through the 70s and 80s. "You decide to try to go in a different direction – and at some later point in time, that will become tradition. The Flying V wasn't tradition in 1958. It was radical."[82]

It is shape that separates those wonderful originals and the modern offshoots from the more traditional and predicatable areas of guitar design. Does shape matter? "Actually," says Matt Masciandaro at ESP, "the sound of a V versus a Strat, for example, is affected less by the body shape and more by the materials used and the method of construction. I've found that many players consider the look and size and weight of these more extreme shapes to be as important as the sound when playing them in a live setting."[83]

"I don't think the shape of a guitar changes things much at all, personally," says Grover Jackson at Reaktor, "other than the psychological state that it might put you in – because you express yourself based on how you feel that you're presenting yourself. But at the end of the day, this is not about us, the people who make this stuff. About the best you can hope to do is to arm somebody with a tool so that they can go do their job and make music."[84]

FLYING V ■ EXPLORER ■ FIREBIRD

How to use the listings

This reference section offers a simple, condensed format to give you information about the Gibson models featured in this book. The following notes are designed to help you use the listing.

At the **head of each entry** or **group of entries** is the **main model name** in bold type, listed in alphabetical order. Under the main model name is the **entry for a single model** or a **group of individual entries**, as appropriate. These entries are presented as one list, in alphanumeric order, with the exception of the Explorer, Flying V, and Firebird lists. The Explorer and Flying V lists are each split into two lists, with Main Models first, in chronological order, followed by Other Models, in alphanumeric order. The Firebird list is split into Reverse-body and Non-reverse-body styles. The alphanumeric order of model names within a group entry is determined by the official name of each model.

After the **model name**, each entry shows a **year or range of years** for the production period of the instrument. These dates, and any other dates shown within this reference section, are approximate. In many cases it's virtually impossible to pinpoint the period during which a model was in production. Gibson's promotional material is usually dated, but the content is often decided far in advance and does not always reflect what was being produced at any given time. Gibson's logs of the total numbers of guitars 'shipped' (which means leaving the factory) sometimes show guitars made in years beyond the range we give for production. Where only a small annual quantity of guitars is shown for a model otherwise produced in reasonably substantial numbers, we assume that these are either samples made before the start of a production period or leftovers sold off after production has ceased. We've tried to list the most accurate dates possible for the production periods of and changes made to these Gibson models, but please treat them as approximate, because that is all they can be.

In italics, following the model name and production year(s), is a brief **one-sentence identification** of the guitar in question. This is intended to help you recognise a specific model at a glance by noting combinations of elements unique to that particular model.

A list of **specification points**, separated into three groups, provides details of the model's features. In the order shown, the points refer to **body**; **neck**; and **electronics**. To avoid repetition, we consider a scale length of 24¾ inches to be common to all models, and humbucking pickups to have covers, unless stated.

At the end of some entries we show **production figures**. For dates until the end of the 70s, we've used official Gibson records that logged the number of guitars shipped from the Kalamazoo factory each year. However, these figures in the listing should be treated with some caution: the calculations were tallied by hand, and human error is evident. The figures we've used here continue to 1979, but we could find no figures for Kalamazoo from 1980 until its closure in 1984, and no figures for any Nashville production since its opening in 1975 until the late 80s – they are apparently lost. The current owners of Gibson are again logging production numbers, but for commercial reasons they will not release that information to us. We have also indicated production numbers for relatively recent Custom Shop limited editions and other small runs where we have this information, but note that the actual number of instruments produced is often less than the officially announced production figure.

Some models were made in a number of **variations**, and where this is so the variations are listed after the specification points, starting with an asterisk (*). Other general comments are also made here.

All this information is designed to tell you more about these Gibson guitars. By using the general information and illustrations earlier in the book, combined with the data in this reference section, you should be able to build up a full picture of any instrument and its pedigree.

REFERENCE: CORVUS / EXPLORER

CORVUS

Corvus I (1982–84)
Body shaped like battle axe, six-on-a-side tuners, bolt-on neck
- Body with cut-out along entire bass side of body, cut-out on upper treble side, deep V-shaped cut-out from bottom end almost to bridge, combination bridge/tailpiece with individual string adjustments, chrome-plated hardware, Silver finish.
- Bolt-on maple neck, unbound rosewood fingerboard, dot inlays, six-on-a-side tuners, decal logo.
- One humbucking pickup with black cover and no visible poles, pickup dipped in epoxy, two knobs.

See also Futura (Corvus-style).
* **Corvus II** (1982–84) Two pickups, three knobs.
* **Corvus III** (1982–84) Three high-output single-coil pickups, two knobs, five-way switch.

EXPLORER

All with:
- Angular body with elongated upper treble bout and lower bass bout.
- Scimitar-shape peghead curves to treble side (a few with V-shape peghead).

EXPLORER MAIN MODELS

Explorer first version (1958–59, 1962–63)
Korina body, knobs in straight line.
- Korina (African limba wood) body, tune-o-matic bridge, stop tailpiece, white pickguard, gold-plated hardware (some nickel-plated 1962–63), Natural finish.
- Unbound rosewood fingerboard, dot inlays.
- Two humbucking pickups, three knobs in straight line, selector switch on treble horn.

Production: 19 (1958); 3 (1959).
1962–63 models assembled from leftover parts.

Explorer second version (1976–79) / **Explorer I** (1981–82) / **Explorer 83** (1983)
Non-korina body, knobs in straight line.
- Mahogany body (limited run with korina body 1976; alder body 1981–83), tune-o-matic bridge, stop tailpiece (optional black Kahler flyer vibrato, other vibratos optional, 1983), white pickguard, chrome-plated hardware; Black, White, or Natural (1975–79) finish.
- Unbound rosewood fingerboard (ebony optional 1983), dot inlays.
- Two humbucking pickups, three knobs in straight line, selector switch on treble horn.

Production: 2 (1975); 2,006 (1976); 1,087 (1977); 274 (1978); 287 (1979).

Explorer third version (1984–89)
Triangular knob configuration, no pickguard
- Alder body (mahogany from 1986), no pickguard, roller drum vibrato (no vibrato from 1987), Black or White finish; optional designer finishes (see Explorer Designer Series in Explorer Other Models).
- Unbound rosewood fingerboard (ebony optional 1984–86, ebony 1987–88, rosewood 1989), decal logo.
- Two humbucking pickups, three knobs in triangular configuration, switch near knobs.

Explorer fourth version / **Explorer Reissue** (1989-90) / **Explorer '76** (1991–2003) / **X-Plorer** (2003–09) / **Explorer** (2009–current)
Pickguard, coverless pickups, three knobs in line
- Mahogany body, tune-o-matic bridge, stop tailpiece, white pickguard (optional mirror pickguard 2000–02), chrome-plated hardware (limited run with pearloid pickguard, gold-plated hardware 1993), Cherry (1989–95, 1998–current), Classic White (1989–current), Ebony (1989–95, 1998–current), Natural (with gold-plated hardware, 1999–2002), Natural Burst (1999–2002), or Vintage Sunburst (1989–93) finish.
- Unbound ebony fingerboard (rosewood optional from 1990).
- Two coverless humbucking pickups, three knobs in straight line, selector switch on treble horn.

EXPLORER OTHER MODELS

Allen Collins Explorer (2003)
Korina body, Maestro vibrato, based on 1958 Explorer, signature model for Lynyrd Skynyrd band member
- Korina body, Maestro vibrato, additional strap button on neck heel, Aged Natural finish, belt buckle wear on back.
- Korina neck, unbound rosewood fingerboard, dot inlays, pearl logo.
- Two humbucking pickups, three knobs in straight line, selector switch on upper horn.

Production: 100.

Eric Clapton Explorer / **Explorer EC** / **Explorer Extra Cut** (2001) Mahogany body, lower bass bout cut off, based on 1958 guitar owned by Clapton, otherwise reissue of Explorer first version. **Production:** 25 (for Japanese market).

EXP 425 *See* Explorer 400.

Explorer Black Hardware (1985) Kahler vibrato standard, black hardware, otherwise same as Explorer fourth version.

Explorer Centennial (April 1994)
Diamond dot on i of logo, package includes 16 x 20 framed photograph and gold signet ring
- Tune-o-matic bridge, stop tailpiece, serial number from

FLYING V ■ EXPLORER ■ FIREBIRD

1894–1994 in raised numerals on tailpiece, numeral *1* of serial number formed by row of diamonds, large white pickguard, gold-plated hardware, Antique Gold finish.
- Bound rosewood fingerboard, dot inlays, pearl logo, letter *i* of logo dotted by inlaid diamond, gold medallion on back of peghead.
- Two humbucking pickups, three knobs, one selector switch.

Production: no more than 101.

Explorer Clapton Cut See Eric Clapton Explorer.

Explorer CMT See The Explorer.

Explorer Designer Series (1984)
Custom graphic finish, pickguard, three knobs in straight line, decal logo
- Finish options:

20: Thin parallel gold stripes on Black, gold-plated hardware.
21: Thin black stripes at right angles on White, chrome-plated hardware.
22: Thin gold stripes at 60-degree angles on White, gold-plated hardware.
Blue Splash: Thick dark blue lines on Alpine White, gold-plated hardware.
Fireworks: Multi-colour pinpoints on Alpine White, chrome-plated hardware.
Galaxy: Lines forming script *Om* and pinpoints on Ebony, chrome-plated hardware.
Lido: Multi-colour lines forming crosses on Alpine White, chrome-plated hardware.
Swirl: Circular lines on ebony, chrome-plated hardware.
Wavelength: Thin multi-colour squiggly lines on Alpine White, chrome-plated hardware.

Explorer EC See Eric Clapton Explorer.

Explorer E/2 (1979–83)
Multi-layer body with bevelled edges
- Five-layer walnut and maple body with walnut or maple top, bevelled body edges, tune-o-matic bridge, TP-6 tailpiece, gold-plated hardware, Natural finish.
- Unbound ebony fingerboard, dot inlays, *E/2* on truss-rod cover.
- Two coverless humbucking pickups, three knobs in straight line, knobs mounted into top, three-way selector switch into pickguard on upper treble horn.

Also known as Explorer E II or Explorer II. See also The Explorer.

Explorer Gothic (1998–2001) / **X-Plorer Gothic** (2001)
Moon and star at twelfth fret
- Tune-o-matic bridge, stop tailpiece, black pickguard, black chrome hardware, Flat Black finish.
- Unbound ebony fingerboard, moon-and-star inlay at twelfth fret (no other inlay), white-outline headstock logo.

- Two coverless humbucking pickups, three knobs in straight line, selector switch on treble horn.

Explorer Heritage (1981–83)
Korina body, black knobs, serial number with 1 prefix
- Reissue of Explorer first version, korina body; Antique Natural, Ebony, or Ivory finish.
- Three-piece korina neck (first eight with one-piece neck), unbound rosewood fingerboard, dot inlays, pearloid keystone tuner buttons, serial number of *1* followed by a space and four digits.
- Two humbucking pickups, three black knobs in straight line.

Production: 100.

Explorer Korina (1982–84)
Korina body, gold knobs, eight-digit serial number
- Reissue of Explorer first version, korina body, Nashville wide-travel tune-o-matic bridge; Candy Apple Red, Ebony, Ivory, or Antique Natural finish.
- Korina neck, unbound rosewood fingerboard, dot inlays, metal tuner buttons, standard eight-digit serial number.
- Two humbucking pickups, three gold knobs in straight line.

Explorer Left Hand (1984–87) Left-handed, otherwise same as Explorer third version.

Explorer Pro (2002–05, 2007–08)
90 percent of standard Explorer size, bound top, bound fingerboard
- Mahogany body (90 percent of standard Explorer size), bound top, tune-o-matic bridge, antique binding, chrome-plated hardware; Ebony or Natural finish.
- Mahogany neck, bound rosewood fingerboard, dot inlays, pearl logo.
- Two coverless humbucking pickups, three knobs in line parallel to edge of guitar, selector switch on treble horn.
* **Explorer Pro Guitar Of The Week** (2007) All-mahogany body, antiqued binding, Cherry finish, Guitar Of The Week. **Production:** 400.
* **Explorer Pro Guitar Of The Week** (2007) Flame maple top, Vintage Sunburst finish. **Production:** 400.
* **Explorer Pro Flamed Maple Top** (2007–08) Flame maple top, Natural Satin or Vintage Sunburst finish.

Explorer Reissue See Explorer fourth version in Explorer Main Models.

Explorer Satin Finish (2003–04) Non-gloss finish, otherwise same as Explorer fourth version.

Explorer Short Vibrola (2007)
Mahogany body, Maestro vibrato
- Mahogany body, Nashville wide-travel tune-o-matic bridge, Maestro vibrola, gold-plated hardware, Trans Amber finish.
- Unbound rosewood fingerboard, dot inlays, pearl logo.

REFERENCE: EXPLORER

- Two humbucking pickups, three knobs in straight line, selector switch on treble horn.

Guitar Of The Week. **Production:** 400.

Explorer Split Headstock See Mahogany Explorer Split Headstock.

Explorer Synthesizer (1985) Roland 700 synthesizer system, Alpine White or Ebony finish.

Explorer Vampire Blood Moon (2011)
Black finish with red filler, red fingerboard markers and switch tip, Schaller vibrato
- Swamp ash body, Schaller vibrato, no pickguard, black hardware, Juju finish (black with red filler).
- Unbound rosewood fingerboard, red "blood drop" inlays, red logo.
- Two active coverless humbucking pickups, three knobs in triangular configuration, switch at treble-side waist.

Explorer Voodoo (2002–04)
Black finish with red filler, voodoo doll fingerboard inlay
- Swamp ash body, tune-o-matic bridge, stop tailpiece, Juju finish (black with red wood filler), black hardware.
- Unbound ebony fingerboard, voodoo doll inlay at fifth fret (no other inlays), red logo.
- Two coverless humbucking pickups with red/black pickup coils, three knobs in straight line, selector switch on treble horn.

Explorer I See Explorer second version in Explorer Main Models.

Explorer II See Explorer E/2.

Explorer III (1984–85)
Three pickups
- Alder body, tune-o-matic bridge, locking nut vibrato system optional, Alpine White or military-style Camouflage finish.
- Maple neck, unbound rosewood fingerboard, dot inlays, metal tuners, decal logo.
- Three soapbar HP-90 pickups, two knobs, two selector switches.
* **Explorer III Black Hardware** (1985) Kahler vibrato standard, black hardware.

Explorer '76 See Explorer fourth version in Explorer Main Models.

Explorer 83 See Explorer second version in Explorer Main Models.

Explorer 90 (1988)
Strings through smaller body, one pickup
- Mahogany body (90 percent of standard Explorer size), tune-o-matic bridge, lightning-bolt tailpiece with strings through body, Floyd Rose vibrato optional, black chrome hardware; Alpine White, Ebony, or Luna Silver finish.
- 25½-inch scale, ebony fingerboard, split-diamond inlays, pearl logo.
- One humbucking pickup, two knobs.

Explorer 90 Double (1988-90)
Strings through smaller body, two pickups
- Mahogany body (90 percent of standard Explorer size), tune-o-matic bridge, lightning-bolt tailpiece with strings through body, Floyd Rose vibrato optional, black chrome hardware; Alpine White, Ebony, or Luna Silver finish.
- 25½-inch scale, ebony fingerboard, split-diamond inlays, pearl logo.
- One single-coil pickup at neck and one humbucking pickup at bridge, two knobs, push/pull volume knob for coil-tap, selector switch between knobs.

Explorer 400 / Explorer 400+ / EXP 425 (1985–86)
One humbucker and two single-coils
- Mahogany body, no pickguard, black hardware, Kahler vibrato, Alpine White, Ebony, Ferrari Red, or Pewter finish.
- Maple neck, unbound ebony fingerboard, dot inlays.
- One coverless Dirty Fingers humbucking pickup and two coverless single-coil pickups, 400-series electronics: master tone and master volume knob, three mini-switches for on/off pickup control, push/pull volume control for coil-tap.

Holy Explorer (2009–current)
Seven cut-outs in body
- Mahogany body, seven holes through body, no pickguard, tune-o-matic bridge, stop tailpiece, chrome-plated hardware, Satin Cherry finish.
- Mahogany neck, rosewood fingerboard, dot inlays, mini-Grover tuners, pearl logo.
- Two coverless humbucking pickups, one knob, one selector switch.

Production: 350.

Mahogany Explorer (2002–03, 2010)
Natural or metallic finish, Custom Shop decal
- Mahogany body, tune-o-matic bridge, stop tailpiece, white pickguard, gold-plated hardware; Natural, Satin Green Metallic, Satin Copper Metallic, Satin Blue Metallic, or Satin Silver Metallic finish.
- Unbound rosewood fingerboard, dot inlays, Custom Shop decal on back of peghead.
- Two humbucking pickups, three knobs in straight line, one selector switch.

Production: 15 in each metallic finish (2002–03); regular production in Natural finish (2010).
* **Mahogany Explorer Split Headstock** (2003–04) V-shaped headstock.

FLYING V ■ EXPLORER ■ FIREBIRD

Reverse Explorer (2008)
Reverse body, lightning bolt pickguard
- Mahogany reverse body with elongated lower treble horn and upper bass horn, black carbon fibre pickguard shaped like lightning bolt, tune-o-matic bridge, stop tailpiece, gold-plated hardware, Antique Walnut finish.
- Unbound rosewood fingerboard, small black dot inlays at frets four and twelve, Moderne-style peghead with tuner posts in curved line.
- Two humbucking pickups, three knobs mounted on pickguard in straight line, selector switch on upper bass horn.

Production: 1,000.

Robot Explorer (2008–current)
Two black knobs and one white knob, trapezoid (crown) inlays, auto-tune feature
- Mahogany body, no pickguard, tune-o-matic bridge, stop tailpiece, chrome-plated hardware, Metallic Red finish.
- Mahogany neck, bound ebony fingerboard, trapezoid (crown) inlays, large tuner housing (servo motors).
- Two coverless humbucking pickups, white pickup mounting rings, knobs in triangular configuration (one white knob controls Robot auto-tuner), switch at treble-side waist.

Limited Run series. **Production:** 350.

Shark Fin (2010)
Rounded cut-out below bridge, peghead points to bass side
- Body shape similar to Explorer with extended lower bass bout but rounded below bridge and truncated lower treble bout, tune-o-matic bridge, stop tailpiece, chrome-plated hardware, Silver Metallic finish.
- Unbound ebony fingerboard, dot inlays, reverse Explorer-style headstock curves to bass side with all tuners on treble side, knurled-knob tuners, black silkscreen logo.
- Two coverless humbucking pickups, two knobs, selector switch between knobs.

Shred X (June 2008)
EMG pickups, no pickguard, no inlays
- No pickguard, Kahler vibrato, black chrome hardware, Ebony finish.
- 50s rounded-neck profile, unbound ebony fingerboard, black dot inlays, locking Grover tuners, pearl logo.
- Two EMG humbucking pickups, three knobs in triangular configuration, switch near waist.

Guitar Of The Month. **Production:** 1,000.

The Explorer / Explorer CMT (1976, 1981–84)
Curly maple top, fine-tune tailpiece
- Maple body, bound curly maple top, tune-o-matic bridge, TP-6 fine-tune tailpiece, gold-plated hardware; Antique Sunburst, Vintage Cherry Sunburst, or Antique Natural finish.
- Maple neck, unbound ebony fingerboard, dot inlays, some with E/2 on truss-rod cover, pearl logo.
- Two coverless Dirty Fingers humbucking pickups, three knobs in straight line, knobs mounted into top, three-way selector switch on upper treble horn.

Tribal Explorer (2009–current)
White finish with black tribal markings, Kahler vibrato
- Mahogany body, Kahler vibrato, no pickguard, black hardware, White finish with black tribal markings.
- Unbound ebony fingerboard, dot inlays, pearl logo.
- Two coverless humbucking pickups, three knobs in triangular configuration, switch at treble-side waist.

Production: 350.

XPL Custom (1985–86)
Body with sharp horns, cut-out in lower treble horn
- Body somewhat similar to Explorer but with sharply pointed horns, cut-out at lower treble horn, bound curly maple top (some with opaque finish and unbound top), locking nut vibrato system, Cherry Sunburst or Alpine White finish.
- Mahogany neck, dot inlays.
- Two coverless Dirty Fingers humbucking pickups, two knobs, one switch.

XPL Standard (1985)
Body shape similar to small Firebird, two coverless humbuckers
- "Sculptured" body edges, small Firebird shape, tune-o-matic bridge or Kahler Flyer vibrato, chrome-plated or black chrome hardware; Ebony, Kerry Green, or Alpine White finish.
- Mahogany neck, dot inlays.
- Two coverless Dirty Fingers humbucking pickups.

X-Plorer *See Explorer fourth version in Explorer Main Models.*

X-Plorer Gothic *See Explorer Gothic.*

X-Plorer New Century (2006–08)
Full body mirror
- Mahogany body, mirror pickguard covers entire body, tune-o-matic bridge, stop tailpiece, chrome-plated hardware.
- Unbound ebony fingerboard, mirror dot inlays, mirror truss-rod cover.
- Two coverless humbucking pickups, three knobs in straight line, selector switch on treble horn.

X-Plorer Studio (2003–04)
90 percent of standard Explorer size, unbound top, unbound fingerboard
- Poplar body (90 percent of standard Explorer size), tune-o-matic bridge, no pickguard; Studio Copper, Metallic Blue, Studio Blue (2003), Metallic Green (2004), or Metallic Yellow (2004) finish.

REFERENCE: EXPLORER / FIREBIRD REVERSE

- Mahogany neck, unbound rosewood fingerboard, dot inlays, pearl logo.
- Two covered mini-humbucking pickups (two coverless humbucking pickups in late 2004), three knobs in line parallel to edge of guitar, selector switch on treble horn.
* **X-Plorer Studio Swamp Ash** (2003–04) Swamp ash body, Natural finish, two coverless humbucking pickups.

7-String Explorer (2009–current)
Seven strings
- Mahogany body, elongated upper treble bout and lower bass bout, tune-o-matic bridge, stop tailpiece, Ebony finish.
- Unbound rosewood fingerboard, no inlays, mini-Grover tuners.
- One active EMG 81-7 pickup and one active EMG 707 pickup, three knobs in straight line.

50th Anniversary 1958 Korina Explorer See 1958 Korina Explorer.

50-Year Commemorative Explorer (October 2008)
Curly maple top, slashed-block inlays
- Curly maple top cap with bevelled edges, no pickguard, tune-o-matic bridge, stop tailpiece, gold-plated hardware, Brimstone Burst finish.
- Bound ebony fingerboard, slashed block inlays, gold fretwire, unbound peghead, *50th* on truss-rod cover, thin script Gibson logo (from early-50s BR-series lap steels), Steinberger gearless tuners.
- Two humbucking pickups, three knobs in straight line, selector switch on treble bout.
Guitar Of The Month. **Production:** 1,000.

1958 Korina Explorer (1993–2008)
Replica of Explorer first version
- Korina body and neck, gold-plated hardware, Antique Natural finish.
- Korina neck, unbound rosewood fingerboard, first eleven numbered with 9 followed by space followed by last digit of year and ranking (9 y### configuration), all with even-numbered ranking: 002, 004, 006, etc; consecutive numbers after 022.
- Two humbucking pickups, three knobs in straight line.
* **50th Anniversary 1958 Korina Explorer** (2008) One-piece korina body, limited run. **Production**: 100.

'84 Explorer (2007)
EMG pickups, white finish, ebony fingerboard
- Tune-o-matic bridge, stop tailpiece, chrome-plated hardware, White finish.
- Unbound ebony fingerboard, dot inlays, pearl logo.
- Two black EMG pickups, three knobs in arc (wide triangular configuration), switch above knobs.
Guitar Of The Week. **Production:** 400.

FIREBIRD

FIREBIRD REVERSE BODY
All with:
- Body with treble (lower) horn larger than bass (upper) horn.

Firebird (1980)
One-piece neck-through-body, dot inlays
- One-piece neck-through-body, tune-o-matic bridge, stop tailpiece; Cherry, Ebony, or Natural finish.
- Dot inlays, reverse peghead with all six tuners on treble side.
- Two mini-humbucking pickups with no polepieces, four knobs, selector switch.

Firebird "medallion" See Firebird V.

Firebird I (1963–65, 1991–92) / **1963 Firebird I** (2000–current)
One mini-humbucker
- Mahogany side wings, three-ply white-black-white pickguard with bevelled edge, red firebird logo on pickguard, wraparound bridge with raised integral saddles, no vibrato (a few with Firebird III vibrato), nickel-plated hardware (gold-plated 1991–92); Sunburst finish or ten custom colours (1963–65): Cardinal Red, Ember Red, Frost Blue, Golden Mist Poly, Heather Poly, Inverness Green Poly, Kerry Green, Pelham Blue Poly, Polaris White, and Silver Mist Poly (Poly = metallic); Vintage Sunburst or 12 custom colours (2000–current): 60s colours plus Faded Cherry, TV Yellow.
- Nine-piece mahogany/walnut neck-through-body, unbound rosewood fingerboard, dot inlays, six tuners all on treble side of peghead (some with tuners on bass side 1965), bevelled peghead edge, Kluson banjo-style tuners, logo on truss-rod cover.
- One mini-humbucking pickup with no polepieces, two knobs.
Production: 80 (1963); 497 (1964); 800 (1965, includes some non-reverse).

Firebird II (1981–82)
Bound maple top, TP-6 tailpiece
- Maple body with bound maple top cap, tune-o-matic bridge, TP-6 fine-tune tailpiece, large backplate for electronics access, Antique Sunburst or Antique Fireburst finish.
- Three-piece maple neck, unbound rosewood fingerboard, dot inlays, decal logo at tip of peghead.
- Two full-size humbucking pickups, active electronics, four black barrel knobs, selector switch, two mini-switches for standard/active and brightness control.

Firebird III (1963–65) / **1964 Firebird III** (2000–current)
Two mini-humbuckers, dot inlays
- Mahogany side wings, three-ply white-black-white

pickguard with bevelled edge, red firebird logo on pickguard, wraparound bridge with raised integral saddles, simple spring vibrato with flat arm; Sunburst finish or ten custom colours (1963–65): Cardinal Red, Ember Red, Frost Blue, Golden Mist Poly, Heather Poly, Inverness Green Poly, Kerry Green, Pelham Blue Poly, Polaris White, and Silver Mist Poly (Poly = metallic); Vintage Sunburst or 12 custom colours (2000–current): 60s colours plus Faded Cherry, TV Yellow.
- Nine-piece mahogany/walnut neck-through-body, single-bound rosewood fingerboard, dot inlays, tuners all on treble side of peghead (all on bass side 1965), Kluson banjo-style tuners (some with right-angle tuners 1965), logo on truss-rod cover.
- Two mini-humbucking pickups with no polepieces, three-way toggle switch.

Production: 272 (1963); 1,124 (1964); 1,020 (1965, includes some non-reverse).

Firebird V (1963–65, 1986–87) / **Firebird Reissue** (1990) / **Firebird V** (1991–current) / **1964 Firebird V** (Custom Shop, 2000–10) / **1965 Firebird V** (2010–current)
Two mini-humbuckers, trapezoid (crown) (crown) inlays
- Mahogany side wings (all-mahogany body with solid finish colours from 2002), three-ply white-black-white pickguard with bevelled edge, red firebird logo on pickguard, tune-o-matic bridge, Deluxe vibrato with metal tailpiece cover engraved with Gibson and leaf-and-lyre (Kahler vibrato or stopbar tailpiece optional 1986–87; no vibrola from 1990); Sunburst or ten custom colours (1963–65): Cardinal Red, Ember Red, Frost Blue, Golden Mist Poly, Heather Poly, Inverness Green Poly, Kerry Green, Pelham Blue Poly, Polaris White, and Silver Mist Poly (Poly = metallic); Vintage Sunburst (1986–current), Classic White (1991–93), Ebony (1991–93), Heritage Cherry (1991–93), or Cardinal Red (1991–93); 12 custom colours (2000–current): 60s colours plus Faded Cherry, TV Yellow.
- Nine-piece mahogany/walnut neck-through-body, single-bound rosewood fingerboard, trapezoid (crown) inlays, tuners all on treble side of peghead (some with all tuners on bass side 1965), Kluson banjo-style tuners (some with right-angle tuners 1965), logo on truss-rod cover.
- Two mini-humbucking pickups with no polepieces, three-way toggle switch.

Production: 62 (1963); 510 (1964), 353 (1965, includes some non-reverse).

* **Firebird V Zebra Wood** (2007) Zebra wood body wings, antiqued inlays and binding, Guitar Of The Week. **Production**: 400.
* **Firebird V Flame Maple** (2007) Flame maple body wings, antiqued inlays and binding, Guitar Of The Week. **Production**: 400.
* **Firebird V Celebrity Series** (1991–93) Black finish, white pickguard, gold-plated hardware.
* **Firebird (V) "medallion"** (1972–73) Limited-edition medallion on top, logo embossed on pickup covers. **Production**: 366.
* **Firebird V Guitar Trader Reissue** (1982–83) Made for Guitar Trader retail store in Red Bank, NJ; banjo tuners, Maestro vibrola, White or Sunburst finish. **Production**: 15.
* **Johnny Winter Signature Firebird V** (2008–09) Replica of Winter's 1963 Firebird V, stopbar tailpiece, holes in top from removal of vibrato, pick wear and arm wear through top finish, belt-buckle wear through back finish, signature and limited-edition number on back of peghead. **Production**: 100.
* **Firebird V 2010** (2010–current) Steinberger tuners.

Firebird V Centennial (July 1994)
Diamond dot on i of logo, package includes 16 x 20 framed photograph and gold signet ring
- Tune-o-matic bridge, stop tailpiece, serial number from 1894–1994 in raised numerals on tailpiece, numeral 1 of serial number formed by row of diamonds, large white pickguard, gold-plated hardware, Sunburst finish.
- Bound ebony fingerboard, pearl block inlays, pearl logo, letter i of logo dotted by inlaid diamond, gold medallion on back of peghead.
- Two mini-humbucking pickups with no polepieces, four knobs, one selector switch.

Production: no more than 101.

Firebird VII (1963–65, 1991–93, 2003–current) / **1965 Firebird VII** (Custom Shop 2000–current)
Three mini-humbuckers, block inlays
- Mahogany side wings (all-mahogany body with red metallic finish 2002–current), three-ply white-black-white pickguard with bevelled edge, red firebird logo on pickguard, tune-o-matic bridge, Deluxe vibrato (tubular lever arm with plastic end cap, metal tailpiece cover engraved with Gibson and leaf-and-lyre decoration, gold-plated hardware (chrome-plated 1991–93); Sunburst or ten custom colours (1963–65): Cardinal Red, Ember Red, Frost Blue, Golden Mist Poly, Heather Poly, Inverness Green Poly, Kerry Green, Pelham Blue Poly, Polaris White, and Silver Mist Poly (Poly = metallic); Frost Blue (1991–93); Vintage Sunburst or 12 custom colours (2000–current): 60s colours plus Faded Cherry, TV Yellow.
- Nine-piece mahogany/walnut neck-through-body, single-bound ebony fingerboard, block inlays beginning at first fret, tuners all on treble side of peghead (all on bass side 1965), bevelled peghead edge, large Kluson banjo-style tuners, logo on truss-rod cover.
- Three mini-humbucking pickups with no polepieces, three-way toggle switch, pearl block inlay (aged inlay 1991–93).

Production: 20 (1963); 173 (1964); 110 (1965, includes some non-reverse).

Firebird Reissue See Firebird V.

REFERENCE: FIREBIRD REVERSE / NON-REVERSE

Firebird Studio (2004–08)
Smaller than standard Firebird
- Mahogany body (shorter than standard Firebird), tune-o-matic bridge, stopbar tailpiece, chrome or gold-plated hardware, Cherry or Ebony finish.
- Set neck, unbound rosewood fingerboard, dot inlays, reverse headstock, logo on truss-rod cover.
- Two full-size humbucking pickups with polepieces, four knobs.

Firebird 76 (1976–78)
Stars on pickguard
- Tune-o-matic bridge, red-and-blue Bicentennial firebird logo (with stars) on pickguard near switch, gold-plated hardware; Sunburst, Natural Mahogany, White, or Ebony finish.
- Neck-through-body, unbound rosewood fingerboard, dot inlays, straight-through banjo tuners with metal buttons.
- Two mini-humbucking pickups with no polepieces, four knobs, selector switch.

Production: 2,847.

Johnny Winter Signature *See* Firebird V.

1963 Firebird I *See* Firebird I.

1964 Firebird III *See* Firebird III.

1964 Firebird V *See* Firebird V.

1965 Firebird V *See* Firebird V.

1965 Firebird VII *See* 1965 Firebird VII.

FIREBIRD NON-REVERSE BODY
All with:
- Body with bass (upper) horn larger than treble (lower) horn.

Firebird I (1965–69)
Two P-90 pickups
- Mahogany body, white pickguard with red firebird logo, wraparound bridge with raised integral saddles, short-arm vibrato with tubular lever and plastic tip; Sunburst or ten custom colours: Cardinal Red, Ember Red, Frost Blue, Golden Mist Poly, Heather Poly, Inverness Green Poly, Kerry Green, Pelham Blue Poly, Polaris White, and Silver Mist Poly (Poly = metallic).
- Set neck, unbound rosewood fingerboard, dot inlays, non-bevelled peghead, right-angle tuners all on bass side of peghead.
- Two black soapbar P-90 pickups, black sliding selector switch, four controls.

Production: 800 (1965, includes some reverse); 1,164 (1966); 200 (1967); 192 (1968); 34 (1969).

Firebird III (1965–69)
Three P-90 pickups
- Mahogany body, white pickguard with red firebird logo, wraparound bridge with raised integral saddles, vibrato with tubular arm; Sunburst or ten custom colours: Cardinal Red, Ember Red, Frost Blue, Golden Mist Poly, Heather Poly, Inverness Green Poly, Kerry Green, Pelham Blue Poly, Polaris White, and Silver Mist Poly (Poly = metallic).
- Set neck, unbound rosewood fingerboard, dot inlays, non-bevelled peghead, right-angle tuners all on bass side of peghead.
- Three black soapbar P-90 pickups, black sliding selector switch, four controls.

Production: 1,020 (1965, includes some reverse); 935 (1966); 463 (1967); 10 (1968); 27 (1969).

Firebird V (1965–69)
Two mini-humbuckers
- Mahogany body, white pickguard with red firebird logo, tune-o-matic bridge, Deluxe vibrato with tubular arm, metal tailpiece cover engraved with Gibson and leaf-and-lyre decoration, nickel-plated hardware; Sunburst or ten custom colours: Cardinal Red, Ember Red, Frost Blue, Golden Mist Poly, Heather Poly, Inverness Green Poly, Kerry Green, Pelham Blue Poly, Polaris White, and Silver Mist Poly (Poly = metallic).
- Set neck, unbound rosewood fingerboard, dot inlays, non-bevelled peghead, right-angle tuners all on bass side of peghead.
- Two mini-humbucking pickups with no polepieces, black sliding selector switch, four controls.

Production: 353 (1965, includes some reverse); 342 (1966); 83 (1967); 50 (1968); 17 (1969).

* **Firebird V 12-string** (1966–67) Symmetrical headstock with centre dip and six tuners per side. **Production:** 248 (1966); 24 (1967).

Firebird VII (1965–69)
Three mini-humbuckers, block inlays
- Mahogany body, white pickguard with red firebird logo, tune-o-matic bridge, Deluxe vibrato with tubular arm, metal tailpiece cover engraved with Gibson and leaf-and-lyre decoration, gold-plated hardware; Sunburst or ten custom colours: Cardinal Red, Ember Red, Frost Blue, Golden Mist Poly, Heather Poly, Inverness Green Poly, Kerry Green, Pelham Blue Poly, Polaris White, and Silver Mist Poly (Poly = metallic).
- Set neck, unbound rosewood fingerboard, dot inlays, non-bevelled peghead, right-angle tuners all on bass side of peghead.
- Three mini-humbucking pickups with no polepieces, black sliding selector switch, four controls.

Production: 110 (1965, includes some reverse); 46 (1966); 9 (1967); 19 (1968); 5 (1969).

* **Firebird Non-Reverse – 3 P-90s** (2003–04) Three soapbar P-90 pickups, Limed TV finish.

Firebird X first version (2010)
Three selector switches, digital electronics, no "X" on fingerboard
- Body shape similar to non-reverse, tune-o-matic bridge, covered stop tailpiece, gold-to-red metallic finish.
- Set neck, unbound fingerboard of highly figured wood, abalone trapezoid (crown) inlays, standard Gibson headstock shape with three tuners per side, bound headstock, oversized truss-rod cover with *Firebird X Limited Edition*, pearl logo.
- Three mini-humbucking pickups with no polepieces, two metal knobs and one lighted bonnet knob for Robot auto-tune control, two switches on lower treble bout, one switch on upper bass horn, digital processor.

Firebird X second version / Firebird X Limited Edition (2011)
Three selector switches, digital electronics, "X" on fingerboard
Similar to Firebird X first version but with maple fingerboard, black dot inlays with *X* at fifth fret, Bluevolution (blue) or Redolution (red) swirl-pattern top finish. **Production:** 1,800.

Non-Reverse Firebird (2002–current)
Two full-size humbuckers or three pickups, dot inlays
- Tune-o-matic bridge, stop tailpiece, gold-plated hardware; Cardinal Red, Walnut, or Phthalo Blue finish (TV White from 2005).
- Set neck, unbound rosewood fingerboard, dot inlay.
- Two full-size humbucking pickups with polepieces (three mini-humbucking pickups with no polepieces or three soapbar P-90 pickups from 2005), four knobs.
* **Non-reverse Firebird Plus (2002)** Two full-size humbuckers with polepieces, some with coil-tap, some with brushed aluminium pickguard, set neck, unbound ebony fingerboard, dot inlay, peghead finish matches body; Blue, Red, or Green Swirl finish. Production: 60 in each finish.

XPL Standard See XPL Standard in Explorer Other Models.

FLYING V
All with:
- V-shaped body
- Triangular peghead shape (except XPL)

FLYING V MAIN MODELS

Flying V first version (1958–59, 1962–63)
Korina body
- Korina (African limba wood) body, body shoulders square at neck, strings anchor through body in V-shaped anchor plate, white pickguard (a few early with black), gold-plated hardware, Natural finish.
- Korina neck, unbound rosewood fingerboard, dot inlays, triangular peghead with rounded top, raised plastic peghead logo.
- Two humbucking pickups, three knobs in straight line, one selector switch.

Production: 81 (1958); 17 (1959).
1962–63 models assembled from leftover parts.

Flying V second version (1967–70)
Mahogany body, vibrato, triangular knob configuration
- Mahogany body, tune-o-matic bridge, Maestro vibrato, large white pickguard, chrome-plated hardware; Natural, Cherry, Black, Candy Apple Red, Pelham Blue, Sparkling Burgundy, or Sunburst finish.
- Unbound rosewood fingerboard, dot inlays, logo on truss-rod cover, most with shorter peghead than Flying V first version (stubby peghead 1970).
- Two humbucking pickups, three "bonnet" knobs ("witch-hat" knobs from 1969) in triangular configuration, one selector switch.

Production: 2 (1966); 111 (1967); 15 (1969); 47 (1970).

Flying V third version "medallion" (1971)
Mahogany body, no vibrato, triangular knob configuration
- Mahogany body with *Limited Edition Reissue* medallion on top, tune-o-matic bridge, stop tailpiece, large white pickguard, chrome-plated hardware, Cherry finish.
- Unbound rosewood fingerboard, dot inlays, logo on truss-rod cover, volute on back of neck, stubby peghead with rounded top.
- Two humbucking pickups, three knobs in triangular configuration, one selector switch.

Production: 350 (1971).

Flying V fourth version (1975–82)
Coverless pickups, triangular knob configuration
- Mahogany body, tune-o-matic bridge, stop tailpiece, large white pickguard, chrome-plated hardware; Natural, Black, Tobacco Sunburst, Candy Apple Red, Bahama Blue, Red, Red Metallic, White, Silver Sky, or Silverburst finish.
- Unbound rosewood fingerboard, dot inlays, logo on truss-rod cover (some with additional decal logo on peghead), short headstock with rounded top.
- Two coverless humbucking pickups, three knobs in triangular configuration, one selector switch below knobs.

Production: 2 (1973); 1 (1974); 1,872 (1975); 423 (1976); 110 (1977); 313 (1978); 778 (1979).

Flying V fifth version (1979)
Bound fingerboard, small block inlays
- Mahogany body, tune-o-matic bridge, stop tailpiece, White finish.
- Bound fingerboard, small block inlays.
- Two humbucking pickups, three knobs in triangular configuration, switch below knobs.

Production: no more than 50.

REFERENCE: FIREBIRD NON-REVERSE / FLYING V

Flying V sixth version (1984–88) / **Flying V 83** (1983)
No pickguard
- Alder body, sloped shoulders, tune-o-matic bridge, stop tailpiece (some with combination bridge/tailpiece 1983; vibrato units optional), no pickguard, chrome-plated hardware; Ebony (1983–88), Ivory (1983–84), Alpine White (1984, 1986–88), Red (1984), Night Violet (with gold-plated hardware, 1985), Scorpions (half white, half black, 1985), Ferrari Red (1985–88), Panther Pink (1985–87), or Pewter (1985–87) finish; optional Designer Series finishes (see Flying V Designer Series in Flying V Other Models).
- Unbound ebony fingerboard (rosewood standard with ebony optional from late 1983), dot inlays, decal logo.
- Two coverless humbucking pickups, three knobs in arc (wide triangular configuration), one selector switch above knobs.

Flying V seventh version / **Flying V Reissue** (1990)
Pickguard, ebony fingerboard, logo on truss-rod cover
- Mahogany body, tune-o-matic bridge, stop tailpiece, large white pickguard, chrome-plated hardware; Cherry, Classic White, Ebony, or Vintage Sunburst finish.
- Unbound ebony fingerboard, dot inlays, logo on truss-rod cover.
- Two coverless humbucking pickups, three knobs in triangular configuration, switch below knobs.

Flying V eighth version / **Flying V '67** (1991–2003) / **X-Factor V** (2003–08) / **Flying V** (2009–current)
Pickguard, ebony fingerboard, logo on peghead
- Mahogany body, tune-o-matic bridge, stop tailpiece, large white pickguard, chrome-plated hardware; Cherry (1991–current), Classic White (1991–current), Ebony (1991–current), Vintage Sunburst (1991–92), Natural (with gold-plated hardware, 1999–current), Natural Burst (1999–2002), Translucent Purple (1999–2002), or Teal (with pearloid pickguard and gold-plated hardware, 1993) finish.
- Unbound ebony fingerboard, dot inlays, decal logo.
- Two coverless humbucking pickups, three knobs in triangular configuration.

FLYING V OTHER MODELS

Cadillac Gold Flying V (1993–94)
Gold finish, large pickguard
- Mahogany body, large pickguard extends to bass edge, tune-o-matic bridge, stop tailpiece, Gold finish.
- Unbound rosewood fingerboard, dot inlays
- Two humbucking pickups, three knobs in triangular configuration, switch and jack below knobs.
Production: 50.
Also known as Gold Flying V.

Flying V Black Hardware (1985) Kahler vibrato standard, black hardware, otherwise same as Flying V seventh version.

Flying V Centennial (July 1994)
Diamond dot on i of logo, package includes 16 x 20 framed photograph and gold signet ring
- Tune-o-matic bridge, stop tailpiece, serial number from 1894–1994 in raised numerals on tailpiece, numeral 1 of serial number formed by row of diamonds, large white pickguard, gold-plated hardware, Antique Gold finish.
- Bound rosewood fingerboard, dot inlays, pearl logo, letter *i* of logo dotted by inlaid diamond, gold medallion on back of peghead.
- Two coverless humbucking pickups, three knobs in triangular configuration, one selector switch.
Production: no more than 101.

Flying V CMT / **The V** (1981–85)
Curly maple top
- Maple body (earliest with mahogany body), curly maple top, no pickguard, bound top, tune-o-matic bridge, vibrato optional, gold-plated hardware; Antique Sunburst, Antique Natural, or Vintage Cherry Sunburst finish.
- Maple neck, unbound ebony fingerboard, dot inlays, pearl logo, short peghead with rounded top.
- Two coverless Dirty Fingers humbucking pickups with cream coils, three knobs in curving line, selector switch between upper knobs.

Flying V Custom (2002, 2004–current)
Five-piece split-diamond headstock inlay
- Mahogany body, multi-ply top binding, V-shaped strings-through tailpiece, gold-plated hardware, Classic White or Faded Cherry finish.
- Bound ebony fingerboard, block inlays, five-piece split-diamond peghead inlay.
- Two humbucking pickups, three knobs in straight line, selector switch on diamond-shaped plate.
Production: 40 (2002).
* **Flying V Custom Stinger** (2003) Custom-ordered by Music Man retailer, various neck dimensions, back of peghead painted black with "stinger" tail, gold-plated hardware; Black, White, Red, or Heritage Cherry finish. Production: 6.

Flying V Designer Series (1984)
Custom graphic finish, no pickguard, three knobs in arc, decal logo
- Finish options:
30: Crisscrossing pinstripes on Black, gold-plated hardware.
31: Black pinstripes divide body into three segments on White, chrome-plated hardware.
32: Black pinstripes form triangle on each fin on Ebony, gold-plated hardware.
Blue Splash: Thick dark blue lines on Alpine White, gold-plated hardware.

Fireworks: Multi-colour pinpoints on Alpine White, chrome-plated hardware.
Galaxy: Lines forming script *Om* and pinpoints on Ebony, chrome-plated hardware.
Lido: Multi-colour lines forming crosses on Alpine White, chrome-plated hardware.
Swirl: Circular lines on Ebony, chrome-plated hardware.
Wavelength: Thin multi-colour squiggly lines on Alpine White, chrome-plated hardware.

Flying V Faded (2009–current) / X-Factor V Faded (2003–08)
Satin cherry finish, large pickguard
- Mahogany body, large pickguard, tune-o-matic bridge, stop tailpiece, Worn Cherry finish.
- Unbound rosewood fingerboard, moon inlays (dots from mid 2003), white truss-rod cover with logo.
- Two coverless humbucking pickups, three knobs in triangular configuration, switch below knobs, jack into pickguard, worn cherry finish.

Flying V Faded Three-Pickup (2007)
Three coverless pickups
- Mahogany body, large pickguard, tune-o-matic bridge, stop tailpiece, Worn Black or Worn White finish
- Unbound rosewood fingerboard, moon inlays (dots from mid 2003), white truss-rod cover with logo.
- Three coverless humbucking pickups, two standard knobs, six-way rotary selector switch with pointer knob

Flying V FF-81 (1981) Made for Frankfurt (Germany) trade show, FF-81 on truss-rod cover, otherwise same specs as Flying V fourth version.

Flying V FF-82 See Flying V Heritage FF-82 in Flying V Heritage entry.

Flying V Figured Top (2003–05)
Figured maple top
- Mahogany body, figured maple top, no pickguard, tune-o-matic bridge, stop tailpiece, nickel-plated hardware, Washed Cherry finish
- Mahogany neck, bound rosewood fingerboard, trapezoid (crown) inlays, Gibson peghead logo and "Flying V" in vertical script on peghead
- Two humbucking pickups, three knobs, one selector switch

Flying V Heritage (1982)
Reissue of 1958 version
- Korina body, tune-o-matic bridge, strings anchor through body in V-shaped tailpiece, gold-plated hardware; Antique Natural, Ebony, Candy Apple Red, or White finish; serial number of letter followed by three digits (example: A 123).
- Three-piece korina neck, unbound rosewood fingerboard, dot inlay, pearl logo.
- Two humbucking pickups, three knobs in straight line, gold knobs.
* **Flying V Heritage FF-82 (1982)** Made for Frankfurt (Germany) trade show, FF-82 on truss-rod cover, eight-digit serial number, otherwise same specs as Flying V Heritage.
* **Flying V Korina (1983)** Black barrel knobs, eight-digit serial number, otherwise same specs as Flying V Heritage.

Flying V Korina See Flying V Heritage.

Flying V Left Hand (1984–87) Left-handed, Ebony or Red finish, otherwise same as Flying V sixth version.

Flying V Limited Custom Shop (1980) Similar to Flying V fourth version with all-Gold finish, oval plaque on back of peghead.

Flying V Mahogany (2001–02) Custom Shop model, similar to 1958 Flying V Korina reissue but with mahogany body and neck, knobs in straight line, gold-plated hardware, Natural finish.

Flying V "medallion" See Flying V third version in Flying V Main Models.

Flying V Mirror Pickguard (2002) Mirror pickguard; Cherry, Ebony, or Classic White finish; otherwise same as '67 Flying V (Flying V eighth version).

Flying V New Century / X-Factor V New Century (2006–08)
Full-body pickguard
- Mahogany body, full-body pickguard, tune-o-matic bridge, stop tailpiece, Ebony finish.
- Unbound ebony fingerboard, mirror dot inlays, large white truss-rod cover with logo.
- Two coverless humbucking pickups, three knobs in triangular configuration.
* **Flying V New Century Guitar Of The Week (2007)** Black carbon fibre full-body pickguard, ebony fingerboard, Satin Ebony finish. Production: 400.

Flying V Primavera (1994)
Primavera (light mahogany) body
- Primavera wood (light mahogany) body, tune-o-matic bridge, stop tailpiece, large pickguard extends to bass edge, gold-plated with Antique Natural finish, chrome-plated hardware with translucent and metallic finishes.
- Unbound rosewood fingerboard, dot inlays, logo on truss-rod cover.
- Two humbucking pickups, three knobs in triangular configuration.

Flying V Quilt Top See Flying V Standard Quilt Top.

REFERENCE: FLYING V

Flying V Reissue See Flying V seventh version in Flying V Main Models.

Flying V Standard Quilt Top (2004–06) Quilted maple top cap, trapezoid (crown) inlay.

Flying V Voodoo (2002)
Black finish with red filler, voodoo doll fingerboard inlay
- Swamp ash body, tune-o-matic bridge, stop tailpiece, Juju finish (black with red wood filler), black hardware.
- Unbound ebony fingerboard, voodoo doll inlay at fifth fret (no other inlays), red logo on truss-rod cover.
- Two coverless humbucking pickups with red/black pickup coils, three knobs in triangular configuration, selector switch below knobs.

Flying V V2 (1979–82)
Boomerang pickups
- Five-layer maple/walnut body with walnut or maple top, bevelled top and back body edges, tune-o-matic bridge, V-shaped tailpiece, gold-plated hardware, Natural finish.
- Unbound ebony fingerboard, dot inlays, V2 on truss-rod cover, short peghead with rounded top.
- Two boomerang-shaped pickups with metal mounting rings, three knobs in straight line, one selector switch.

Also known as Flying V II.

Flying V XPL (1984–86)
Explorer-style scimitar headstock
- Mahogany body, Kahler vibrato or combination bridge/tailpiece with individual string adjustments (tune-o-matic optional from 1985), chrome-plated hardware; Alpine White, Ebony, Ferrari Red, Night Violet, Pewter, Plum Wineburst, Red, or Regal Blue finish.
- Maple neck, unbound ebony fingerboard, Explorer-style peghead, six-on-a-side tuner arrangement.
- Two coverless humbucking pickups, three knobs in triangular configuration, switch above knobs.
* **Flying V XPL Black Hardware** (1985) Black hardware, Kahler vibrola standard; Ebony, Alpine White, or Red finish.

Flying V I (1981)
Block inlays, unbound fingerboard
- Tune-o-matic bridge, stop tailpiece (several vibrato systems optional), large pickguard, chrome-plated hardware, White finish.
- Unbound ebony fingerboard, block inlays, logo on truss-rod cover, short peghead with rounded top.
- Two coverless humbucking pickups, three knobs in triangular configuration, selector switch below knobs.

Flying V II See Flying V V2.

Flying V '67 See Flying V eighth version in Flying V Main Models.

Flying V 83 See Flying V sixth version in Flying V Main Models.

Flying V 90 (1988)
Split-diamond inlays, one pickup
- Mahogany or alder body, tune-o-matic bridge, stop tailpiece, small black pickguard, Floyd Rose vibrato optional, black chrome hardware; Alpine White, Ebony, or Nuclear Yellow finish.
- 25½-inch scale, unbound ebony fingerboard, split-diamond inlays, pearl logo.
- One humbucking pickup, one knob.
* **Flying V 90 Golden Eagle** (1989) V-shaped tailpiece, gold truss-rod cover, vertical headstock logo, eagle peghead graphic, Black & Gold finish with simulated gold feathers.

Flying V 90 Double (1989-90)
Split-diamond inlays, two pickups
- Mahogany or alder body, tune-o-matic bridge, stop tailpiece, small black pickguard, Floyd Rose vibrato optional, black chrome hardware; Alpine White, Ebony, or Luna Silver finish.
- 25½-inch scale, unbound ebony fingerboard, split-diamond inlays, pearl logo.
- One humbucking pickup and one single-coil pickup, two knobs, push/pull volume knob for coil-tap.

Flying V '98 (1998, 2002)
Three knobs in straight line, Limited Edition decal on back of headstock
- Mahogany body, tune-o-matic bridge, stop tailpiece, small pickguard, gold-plated hardware with Natural or Natural Burst finish, chrome-plated hardware with Translucent Purple finish.
- Unbound rosewood fingerboard, dot inlays, Limited Edition decal on back of headstock, white truss-rod cover with gold logo, Grover tuners with metal buttons.
- Two coverless ceramic-magnet humbucking pickups, three knobs in straight line, switch above knobs, jack in lower treble bout.

Flying V '98 Gothic (1998–2001)
Black finish, moon-and-star at twelfth fret
- Tune-o-matic bridge, stop tailpiece, black pickguard, black chrome hardware, Satin Ebony finish.
- Unbound ebony fingerboard, moon-and-star inlay at twelfth fret, no other inlay, white outline of logo on peghead,
- Two coverless '57 Classic humbucking pickups, three knobs in straight line, switch above knobs, jack in lower treble bout

Flying V 400 / Flying V 400+ (1985–86)
One humbucker and two single-coil pickups
- Kahler Flyer vibrato, black chrome hardware; Alpine White,

FLYING V ■ EXPLORER ■ FIREBIRD   129

Ebony, Ferrari Red, or Pewter finish.
- Unbound fingerboard, dot inlays.
- One Dirty Fingers humbucking pickup and two single-coil pickups, 400-series electronics: master tone and master volume knob, three mini-switches for on/off pickup control, push/pull volume control for coil-tap.

Gold Flying V See Cadillac Gold Flying V.

Holy V (January 2009)
Three holes in body
- Mahogany body, triangular hole through body in each wing, boomerang-shaped hole between pickup and fingerboard, chrome-plated hardware, Natural finish.
- Bound ebony fingerboard, split-diamond inlays, Gibson logo on truss-rod cover, Steinberger Gearless tuners.
- One coverless humbucking pickup, one knob.

Guitar Of The Month. **Production:** 1,000.

Jimi Hendrix Psychedelic Flying V (2006)
Psychedelic finish
- Based on 1967 version hand-painted by Hendrix, Maestro vibrato, large white pickguard, chrome-plated hardware, Oxblood Psychedelic finish.
- Mahogany neck, unbound rosewood fingerboard, dot inlays, long peghead.
- Two humbucking pickups, three black "witch hat" knobs in triangular configuration, selector switch below knobs.

Inspired By limited-run series. Production: 150.

Jimi Hendrix '69 Flying V Custom (1991–93, 1995)
Hendrix signature on pickguard, based on 1969 model
- Mahogany body, tune-o-matic bridge, stop tailpiece, large white pickguard with Hendrix signature on bass side of bridge, gold-plated hardware, Ebony finish.
- Mahogany neck, bound rosewood fingerboard, split-diamond inlays, truss-rod cover with limited-edition number, pearl logo, Hall Of Fame logo on back of headstock.
- Two humbucking pickups, three knobs in triangular configuration.

Production: 400, numbered on truss-rod cover (1991–93); 25 un-numbered (promotional for RCA Records, 1995).

Judas Priest Flying V (2005)
Candy Apple Red finish, tune-o-matic with nylon saddles
- Mahogany body, tune-o-matic bridge with nylon saddles, Candy Apple Red finish with Custom Authentic aging treatment, certificate signed by KK Downing and Glenn Tipton.
- Unbound rosewood fingerboard, dot inlay, long headstock.
- Two coverless 57 Classic humbuckers, three knobs in triangular configuration.

Production: 30 (sold as a set with Judas Priest SG).

Lenny Kravitz 1967 Flying V (2001–04)
Mirror pickguard, black sparkle finish
- Mahogany body, tune-o-matic bridge, Maestro vibrato, mirror pickguard, Black finish with sparkles, Maestro vibrato.
- Unbound rosewood fingerboard, dot inlays, mirror truss-rod cover.
- Two humbucking pickups, three knobs in triangular configuration, one selector switch.

Production: 125.

Lonnie Mack Flying V (1993–94)
Bigsby vibrato between body wings
- Mahogany body, tune-o-matic bridge, Bigsby vibrato with anchor bar between body wings, Cherry finish.
- Unbound rosewood fingerboard, dot inlays, moulded plastic peghead logo.
- Two humbucking pickups, three knobs in straight line.

Production: 195.

Mahogany Flying V (2002–04) Mahogany neck and body; Satin Green Metallic, Satin Copper Metallic, Satin Blue Metallic, or Satin Silver Metallic finish. Production: 15 in each finish.

Reverse Flying V (2007–08)
Reverse body with V opening toward neck
- Mahogany reverse body (V opens toward neck), tune-o-matic bridge, V-shaped strings-through tailpiece with point at bottom, gold-plated hardware; Classic White, Ebony, or Natural finish.
- Unbound ebony fingerboard, dot inlays, asymmetrical V-shaped headstock.
- Two humbucking pickups, one knob, selector switch on treble horn.

Production: 300 in each colour.
* **Reverse Flying V Guitar Of The Week** (2007) Trans Amber finish. Production: 400.

Robot Flying V (2008–current)
One black knob and one white knob, trapezoid (crown) inlays, auto-tune feature
- Mahogany body, no pickguard, tune-o-matic bridge, stop tailpiece, chrome-plated hardware, Metallic Red finish.
- Mahogany neck, bound ebony fingerboard, trapezoid (crown) inlays, large tuner housing (servo motors).
- Two coverless humbucking pickups, white pickup mounting rings, two knobs (one white knob controls Robot auto-tuner), switch above knobs, jack next to lower knob.

Rudolf Schenker Flying V (1993)
White finish on bass side, black finish on treble side, signature on pickguard
- Mahogany body, tune-o-matic bridge, stop tailpiece, large

REFERENCE: FLYING V

white pickguard with Schenker signature, White & Black finish (white bass side, black treble side).
- Black and white headstock, Custom Shop decal on back of headstock.
- Two coverless humbucking pickups, three knobs in triangular configuration.

Production: 103.

Scorpions Flying V (1993)
White finish on bass side, black finish on treble side, no pickguard
- Mahogany body, tune-o-matic bridge, stop tailpiece, White & Black finish (white bass side, black treble side).
- Custom Shop decal on back of headstock.
- Two coverless humbucking pickups, three knobs in triangular configuration.

Shred V (August 2008)
Black finish, black dot inlays
- Mahogany body, no pickguard, Kahler vibrato, black chrome hardware, Ebony finish.
- 50s rounded neck profile, unbound ebony fingerboard, black dot inlays, locking Grover tuners.
- Two EMG humbucking pickups, two knobs, selector switch above knobs, jack to side of lower knob.

Guitar Of The Month. **Production**: 1,000.

The V *See* Flying V CMT.

Tribal V (2009–10)
White finish with black tribal markings, Kahler vibrato
- Mahogany body, Kahler vibrato, no pickguard, black hardware, White finish with black tribal markings.
- Unbound ebony fingerboard, dot inlays, white tribal graphic on peghead.
- Two coverless humbucking pickups, two knobs, one selector switch above knobs, jack to right of lower knob.

Limited Run series. **Production**: 350.

X-Factor V *See* Flying V eighth version in Flying V Main Models.

X-Factor V Faded *See* Flying V Faded.

X-Factor V New Century *See* Flying V New Century.

Zakk Wylde Flying V Bullseye (2008–09) / **Zakk Wylde Flying V Custom Floyd Rose** (2010–current)
Bullseye finish
- Mahogany body, Floyd Rose vibrato, black and white bullseye graphic on body.
- Bound ebony fingerboard, pearl block inlay, bound peghead, five-piece split-diamond peghead inlay, pearl logo.
- Two EMG humbucking pickups, four knobs, selector switch.

Zakk Wylde ZV Buzzsaw (2008–09)
Buzzsaw finish, Flying V lower bout with SG upper bout
- Mahogany body merging Flying V lower-bout legs with SG upper-bout horns, tune-o-matic bridge, V-shape tailpiece, Ebony finish with orange buzzsaw motif.
- Bound ebony fingerboard, pearl block inlay, bound peghead, five-piece split-diamond peghead inlay, pearl logo.
- Two EMG humbucking pickups, three knobs, selector switch.

Inspired By limited-run series. **Production**: 100.

40th Anniversary Flying V (1998)
Coverless pickups, knobs in straight line
- Mahogany body, tune-o-matic bridge, stop tailpiece, gold-plated hardware with Antique Natural finish, chrome-plated hardware with Tobacco Burst or Translucent Purple finish.
- Unbound rosewood fingerboard, dot inlays, logo on truss-rod cover.
- Two coverless ceramic-magnet humbucking pickups, three knobs in straight line.

50th Anniversary Korina Flying V (2008)
Korina body, black pickguard
- Korina body, tune-o-matic bridge, V-shaped tailpiece with strings-through, black pickguard, gold-plated hardware, Natural finish.
- Korina neck, unbound rosewood fingerboard, dot inlays, raised plastic peghead logo.
- Two humbucking pickups, three black bonnet-shaped knobs in straight line, selector switch above knobs.

Production: 100.

50-Year Commemorative Flying V (March 2008)
Curly maple top cap with bevelled edges, slashed-block inlays
- Mahogany body, curly maple top cap with bevelled edges, tune-o-matic bridge, stop tailpiece, gold-plated hardware, Brimstone Burst finish.
- Bound ebony fingerboard, slashed-block inlays, gold fretwire, bound peghead, *50th* on truss-rod cover, inverted red V on peghead, banjo-style tuners, thin script Gibson logo (from early-50s BR-series lap steels), Steinberger gearless tuners.
- Two humbucking pickups, two knobs, selector switch below knobs.

Guitar Of The Month. **Production**: 1,000.

1958 Korina Flying V (1991–2009) / **1959 Korina Flying V** (2010–current)
Replica of Flying V first version
- Korina body, tune-o-matic bridge, V-shaped strings-through tailpiece, gold-plated hardware, Antique Natural finish.
- Korina neck, unbound rosewood fingerboard, dot inlays, first eleven examples numbered with 9 followed by space followed by last digit of year and ranking (9 y###

FLYING V ■ EXPLORER ■ FIREBIRD

configuration), all with uneven-numbered ranking: 001, 003, 005, etc; consecutive numbers after 022.
- Two humbucking pickups, three knobs in straight line.
* **1958 Flying V Split Headstock** (2004) Split headstock shape.
* **1958 Flying V Split Headstock Mahogany** (2004) Mahogany body and neck, split headstock shape.

'59 Flying V Standard Quilt Top (2004–06)
Maple top and peghead veneer
- Quilted maple top cap, tune-o-matic bridge, V-shaped strings-through tailpiece, black pickguard, Cherry finish on top and neck, Black finish on back.
- Maple neck, unbound rosewood fingerboard, dot inlays, maple peghead veneer, moulded plastic logo.
- Two humbucking pickups, three knobs in straight line.

'67 Flying V Reissue (2002–03, 2009) Reissue of Flying V version two, Maestro vibrato, nickel-plated hardware; Antique Natural, Classic White, Ebony, Faded Cherry, or Tobacco Sunburst finish

'69 Flying V Custom *See* Jimi Hendrix '69 Flying V Custom.

'84 Flying V (2007) Two coverless humbucking pickups, two knobs, Silverburst finish; Guitar Of The Week. Production: 400.

FUTURA [Corvus-style]
Futura (1982–84)
Body shaped like battle axe, six-on-a-side tuners, neck-through-body
- Neck-through-body, cut-out along entire bass side of body, cut-out on upper treble side, deep cut-out from bottom end almost to bridge, Gibson/Kahler Supertone vibrato optional, large tailpiece with individually adjustable saddles, gold-plated hardware; Ebony, Ultra Violet, or Pearl White finish.
- Rosewood fingerboard, dot inlays, six-on-a-side tuners.
- Two humbucking pickups with black covers and no visible poles, two knobs.

See also Corvus.

FUTURA [Explorer-style]
Futura Reissue (1996) / **Mahogany Futura** (2002–04)
Explorer-like body, V-shaped peghead (reissue of Explorer prototype)
- Mahogany body, body shape similar to Explorer but with sharper angles, narrower treble horn, narrower waist; Natural (1996), Satin Green Metallic (2002–04), Satin Copper Metallic (2002–04), Satin Blue Metallic (2002–04), or Satin Silver Metallic (2002–04) finish.

- Unbound rosewood fingerboard, dot inlays, V-shaped peghead.
- Two humbucking pickups, three knobs.

Production: 100 (1996); 15 in each of four metallic colours (2002–04).

MODERNE
Moderne Heritage (1982–83)
Asymmetrical body with offset V at base, wide flared headstock
- Korina body with scooped treble side, tune-o-matic bridge, Natural finish.
- Unbound rosewood fingerboard, dot inlays, string guides on peghead, serial number of letter followed by three digits.
- Two humbucking pickups, three barrel knobs, gold-plated hardware.

RD
All with:
- Double-cutaway maple body, with upper treble horn longer than upper bass horn and lower bass horn larger than lower treble horn.

RD Artist (1977–79) / **RD Artist/77** (1980) / **RD** (1981)
Winged-f on peghead
- Tune-o-matic bridge, TP-6 tailpiece, large backplate, gold-plated hardware; Antique Sunburst, Ebony, or Natural finish (also Fireburst 1977–79).
- Three-piece mahogany neck, unbound ebony fingerboard (bound from 1978), 24¾-inch scale (25½ from 1978), block inlays, multiple-bound peghead, winged-*f* peghead inlay, pearl logo.
- Two humbucking pickups, active electronics, four knobs (standard Gibson controls), three-way pickup selector switch, three-way switch for mode selection (neutral, bright, front pickup expansion with back pickup compression; two two-way switches from 1978).

Production: 2,340 (1977–79).
* **RD Artist/79** (1980) 24¾-inch scale.

RD Artist CMT (1981)
Curly maple top
- Bound curly maple top, TP-6 fine-tune tailpiece, chrome-plated hardware, Antique Cherry Sunburst or Antique Sunburst finish.
- Maple neck, bound ebony fingerboard, block inlays.
- Two humbucking pickups, three gold speed knobs.

Production: 100.

RD Custom (1977–78) / **77 Custom** (1979)
Maple fingerboard

REFERENCE: FUTURA / MODERNE / RD / SERIAL NUMBERS

- Tune-o-matic bridge, chrome-plated hardware, large backplate, Natural or Walnut finish.
- 25½-inch scale, maple fingerboard, dot inlays, model name on truss-rod cover, decal logo.
- Two humbucking pickups, active electronics, four knobs (standard Gibson controls), three-way pickup selector switch, two-way mini switch for mode selection (neutral or bright).

Production: 1,498 (1977–79).

RD Standard (1977–78)
Rosewood fingerboard, dot inlays
- Tune-o-matic bridge, chrome-plated hardware; Natural, Tobacco Sunburst, or Walnut finish.
- 25½-inch scale, rosewood fingerboard, dot inlays, model name on truss-rod cover, decal logo.
- Two humbucking pickups, four knobs, one selector switch.

RD Standard Reissue (2007)
Silverburst finish
- Tune-o-matic bridge, stop tailpiece, black pickguard, chrome-plated hardware, Silverburst finish.
- 25½-inch scale, unbound ebony fingerboard, dot inlays, plain truss-rod cover, Grover Rotomatic tuners.
- Two coverless Dirty Fingers humbucking pickups, three knobs, one selector switch.

Guitar Of The Week. **Production:** 400.

SERIAL NUMBERS

NUMBER INK-STAMPED ON BACK OF PEGHEAD

1. Configuration: # ####

1958–60
Code: y nnnn
y = last digit of year, 1958–60
nnnn = ranking among solidbody models
Example: 8 1234 = 1958

1982–83
Code: 1 nnnn
1 = Heritage Explorer
nnnn = ranking

Late 1992–current, reissues of 1957–59 models,
Code: m ynnn
m = model code
y = last digit of year of manufacture
nnn = ranking
Model code: 7 = 1957 Futura; 8 = 1958 Explorer; 9 = 1959 Flying V
Example: 9 8345 = Flying V reissue, 1998 or 2008

2. Configuration: #-9### or #-9####

Late 1992–current, Custom Shop non-reissues
Code: y-9nnn or, if ranking exceeds 999, y-9nnnn
y = last digit of year
9 = designation for Custom Shop guitar
nnn(n) = ranking

3. Configuration: A ### (letter ranging from A to K)

Late 1981–83
Code: A nnn
Letter A–K = Heritage Flying V or Moderne
nnn = ranking.
Most series return to 001 after 099 (example: A 098, A 099, B 001, B 002, etc), but some examples have ranking of 100 and higher.

4. Configuration: ## ####

70s and 80s, special runs
Code: yy nnnn
yy = year
nnnn = ranking

5. Configuration: ####-##

1994, Centennial models
Code: yyyy-mm
yyyy = ranking of the model according to years of the centennial (1894 corresponds to #1, 1994 corresponds to #101)
mm = month of the model within the series, ranging from 1–14 (only twelve models were actually produced; two more were prototyped)

6. Configuration: CS### or CS####

1993-current, Custom Shop models

FLYING V ■ EXPLORER ■ FIREBIRD

133

NUMBER PRESSED INTO BACK OF PEGHEAD

1. Six digits, no "MADE IN USA"
1963–70

Many numbers from 1963–69 appear on more than one instrument. This list was originally compiled by André Duchossoir from Gibson records.

RANGE	YEAR
61450–64222	1963
64240–71040	1964
71041–96600	1962, a few from 1963, 1964
96601–99999	1963
000001–099999	1967
100000–106099	1963, 1967
106100–106899	1963
109000–109999	1963, 1967
110000–111549	1963
111550–115799	1963, 1967
115800–118299	1963
118300–120999	1963, 1967
121000–139999	1963
140000–140100	1963, 1967
140101–144304	1963
144305–144380	1964
144381–149864	1963
149865–149891	1964
149892–152989	1963
152990–174222	1964
174223–176643	1964, 1965
176644–250335	1964
250336–305983	1965
306000–310999	1965, 1967
311000–320149	1965
320150–320699	1967
320700–329179	1965
329180–330199	1965, 1967
330200–332240	1965, 1967–68
332241–348092	1965
348093–349100	1966
349121–368638	1965
368640–369890	1966
370000–370999	1967
380000–385309	1966
390000–390998	1967
400001–406666	1966
406667–409670	1966–68
409671–410900	1966
410901–419999	no entries in ledger
420000–429193	1966
500000–500999	1965–66, 1968–69
501009–501600	1965
501601–501702	1968
501703–502706	1965, 1968
503010–503109	1968

RANGE	YEAR
503405–520955	1965, 68
520956–530056	1968
530061–530850	1966, 1968–69
530851–530993	1968–69
530994–539999	1969
540000–540795	1966, 1969
540796–545009	1969
555000–556909	1966
558012–567400	1969
570087–570643	1966
570645–570755	1966–67
570857–570964	1966
580000–580080	1969
180086–580999	1966–67, 1969
600000–600998	low-end models, 1966, some 1967, 1968
600000–606090	high-end models, 1969
700000–700799	1966–67
750000–750999	1968–69
800000–800999	1966–69
801000–812838	1966, 1969
812900–819999	1969
820000–820087	1966, 1969
820088–823830	1966
824000–824999	1969
828002–847488	1966, 1969
847499–858999	1966, 1969
859001–895038	1967, 1969
895039–896999	1968
897000–898999	1967, 1969
899000–899999	1968
900000–901999	1970
910000–999999	1968

2. Six digits, "MADE IN USA" stamped below number
1970–75

RANGE	YEAR
6 digits + A	1970
000000s	1973
100000s	1970–75
200000s	1973–75
300000s	1974–75
400000s	1974–75
500000s	1974–75
600000s	1970–72, 1974–75
700000s	1970–72
800000s	1973–75
900000s	1970–72

Late 1997–current, Custom Shop reissues of 1963–69 guitars
Code: yynnnm
yy = year
nnn = ranking
m = model code
Model code: 3 = 1963 Firebird I; 4 = 1964 Firebird III; 5 = 1965 Firebird V and VII; 7 = 1967 Flying V

REFERENCE: SERIAL NUMBERS / CHRONOLOGY

3. Eight or nine digits

1977–current. Beginning in 2008, most Gibsons have the year stamped below "MADE IN USA" on the back of the headstock.

Code: ydddynnn or, beginning July 2005, ydddybnnn
yy (first and fifth digits) = year of manufacture
ddd (digits 2–4) = day of the year; 001 = January 1, 365 = December 31
b = batch number, from 0–9; batches are 200 instruments (rankings go from 500–699, then batch number increases and ranking reverts to 500)
nnn (digits 6–8) = rank of the instrument that day. Serial-number stamp is applied in mid-production, at the point when the neck is attached to the body. All instruments made at the Kalamazoo factory (1977–84) were numbered beginning with 001 each day. Instruments made at the Nashville factory from 1977–89 were numbered each day beginning with 500 or 501. Beginning in 1990, regular production models continued to be numbered in Nashville each day beginning with 500 or 501, but some models were also numbered in the 300s, 400s, 700s, 800s and 900s.
Examples:
80012005 = the fifth instrument made in Kalamazoo on the first day of 1982
0256702525 = the 125th instrument made in the second batch (the 325th instrument of the day) in Nashville on the 256th day of 1990
Exception: configuration 94##### = 1994.

4. Number on decal

1975–77
Configuration: ## ###### with two-number prefix in smaller type size)
Prefix code: 99 = 1975; 00 = 1976; 06 = 1977

Chronology

Explorer (1958–59, 1962–63)
Flying V first version (1958–59, 1962–63)

Firebird I reverse body (1963–65, 1991–92)
Firebird III reverse body (1963–65)
Firebird V reverse body (1963–65, 1986–87)
Firebird VII reverse body (1963–65, 1991–93, 2003–current)

Firebird I non reverse body (1965–69)
Firebird III non reverse body (1965–69)
Firebird V non reverse body (1965–69)
Firebird VII non reverse body (1965–69)
Firebird V 12-string non reverse body (1966–67)
Flying V second version (1967–70)

Flying V third version "medallion" (1971)
Firebird (V) / Firebird Medallion (1972–73)
Flying V fourth version (1975–82)
Explorer second version (1976–79)
The Explorer / Explorer CMT (1976, 1981–84)
Firebird 76 (1976–78)
RD Artist (1977–79)
RD Custom (1977–78)
RD Standard (1977–78)
Explorer E/2 (1979–83)

Flying V V2 (1979–82)
Flying V fifth version (1979)
77 Custom (RD) (1979)
Firebird (1980)
Flying V Limited Custom Shop (1980)
RD Artist/77 (1980)
RD Artist/79 (1980)
Explorer Heritage (1981–83)
Explorer I (1981–82)
Firebird II (1981–82)
Flying V CMT / The V (1981–85)
Flying V FF-81 (1981)
Flying V I (1981)
RD (1981)
RD Artist CMT (1981)
Corvus I (1982–84)
Corvus II (1982–84)
Corvus III (1982–84)
Explorer Korina (1982–84)
Firebird V Guitar Trader Reissue (1982–83)
Flying V Heritage (1982)
Flying V Heritage FF-82 (1982)
Futura (1982–84)
Moderne Heritage (1982–83)
Explorer 83 (1983)
Flying V Korina (1983)
Flying V 83 (1983)
Explorer Designer Series (1984)
Explorer Left Hand (1984–87)
Explorer third version (1984–89)
Explorer III (1984–85)

FLYING V ■ EXPLORER ■ FIREBIRD

F

Fender, 11, 13, 14, 16, 20, 23, 28, 37, 40, 41, 43, 44, 96, 107
Fernandes, 34
Firewind, 114

G

G., Gus, *111*, 114, 115
Geib (case maker), 18, 25
Gibbons, Billy, 33, 45, *47*, 48
Gibson
   Corvus models, 101, *102–103*, 119
   Custom Shop, 108
   dates of production, 118
   and ESP lawsuit, 105
   Explorer models
      Allen Collins, 112, 119
      Black Hardware, 119
      Centennial, 119
      CMT, 122
      Designer Series, 104, 106, 120
      E II, *see* E/2
      E/2, 96, 99, 120
      EC, 119
      Eric Clapton, 88, 90, 119
      EXP-425, 121
      Extra Cut, 119
      Gothic, 120
      Guitar Of The Month, 122, 123
      Guitar Of The Week, 120, 121, 123
      Heritage, 97, 120
      Holy, 121
      Korina, 120
      Left Hand, 120
      Mahogany, 121
      Pro, 120
      Reissue, 119
      Reverse, 122
      Robot, 113, 122
      Satin Finish, 120
      Shark Fin, 122
      Short Vibrola, 120
      Shred X, 122
      Synthesizer, 104, 121
      The Explorer, 122
      Tribal, 122
      Vampire Blood Moon, 113, 121
      Voodoo, 121
      XPL, 104, 122
      X-Plorer, 119, 120, 122
      I, 119
      II, *see* E/2
      III, 121

7-String, 123
50-Year Commemorative, 123
50s original (first version), *26–27*, *30–31*, 31, *78–79*, *90*
   copies of, 80
   design, 28, 37
   history, 16, 17, 25, 29
   influence on other makers, 72, 73, 76, 81
   and musicians, 48, 58, 64, 67, 76, 88
   patent, 16, 17, *27*
   reference entry, 119
   shipping totals, 32
   60s leftovers, 31, 32
   split headstock, 16, 17, 26, 28, 84, 88
50th Anniversary, 123
'76 original (second version), 89, 104, *106–107*, 112, 119
'83, 119
'84, 123
'84 original (third version), 104, 119
'90, 121
90s reissue of 50s-style, *see* 1958 Korina
400, 104, 121
1958 Korina (reissue), 109, 123
Firebird
   custom colours, 38, 41, 43, 65
   named, 36
   non-reverse models, 42, 43, 44, 45, 48, 64, 125–126
      Non-Reverse, 125, 126
      X, 113, 126
      I original, *42–43*, 125
      II, 125
      III original, *42–43*, 125
      V original, 125
      V 12-string, 125
      VII original, 51, 125
   reverse-body models, 37, 38, 40, 41, 44, 48, 56, 64, 65, 88, 89, 112, 113, 123–125
      Celebrity Series (V), 124
      Firebird, 123
      Guitar Of The Week, 124
      Guitar Trader Reissue (V), 124
      Johnny Winter (V), 112, 124
      Medallion (V), 124
      Reissue (V), 124
      Studio, 125
      through-neck, 37, 44
      I original, 123
      II, 123

      III original, 123
      V Centennial, 124
      V original, *38–39*, *66*, 124
      V 2010, 124
      VII original, *39*, *70–71*, 124
      '76, 89, 91, 125
      1963 I, 123
      1964 III, 123
      1964 V, 124
      1965 V, 124
      1965 VII, 124
   Flying V models
      Black Hardware, 127
      Cadillac Gold, 127
      Centennial, 127
      CMT, 127
      Custom, 127
      Designer Series, 104, 106, 127
      Double, 104, 129
      Faded, 113, 128
      FF-81, 128
      FF-82, *see* Heritage
      Figured Top, 128
      Gold, 127
      Golden Eagle, 129
      Gothic, 129
      Guitar Of The Month, 130, 131
      Guitar Of The Week, 128, 130, 132
      Heritage, 97, 100, 103, 128
      Holy, 130
      Jimi Hendrix Psychedelic, 130
      Jimi Hendrix '69 Custom, 112, 130
      Judas Priest, 61, 130
      Korina, 128
      Left Hand, 128
      Lenny Kravitz 1967, 112, 130
      Limited Custom Shop, 128
      Lonnie Mack, 112, 130
      Mahogany, 128, 130
      Medallion (third version), *51*, 53, 56, 60, 61, 69, 126
      Mirror Pickguard, 128
      New Century, 128
      Primavera, 128
      Quilt Top, 128, 129
      Reissue, 127
      Reverse, 130
      Robot, 113, 130
      Rudolf Schenker, 112, 130
      Scorpions, 112, 131
      Shred, 131
      Split Headstock, 132
      The V, 127
      Tribal, 131
      Voodoo, 129

INDEX

V II, *see* V2
V2, 96, 97, *98-99*, 129
X-Factor, 127, 128
XPL, 104, 129
Zakk Wylde, 96, 131
I, 129
40th Anniversary, 131
50-Year Commemorative, 131
50s original (first version), *22-23, 47, 50-51*
   Cadillac V tailpiece, 17, 25
   case, *22*
   control layout, 24
   copies of, 80
   design, 21, 24
   history, 15, 17, 18, 19, 20, 28
   influence on other makers, 81
   and musicians, 8, 45, 46, 47, 48, 50, 57, 59, 77, 79
   named, 19
   patent, 15, 17, *23*
   prototype, 18
   reference entry, 126
   shipping totals, 29
   60s leftovers, 32
   store displays, *31*, 32
50th Anniversary Korina, 131
'59 Standard Quilt Top, 132
'67, 127
'67 original (second version), *54-55, 62-63*
   copies of, 80
   Hendrix 'psychedelic' guitar, 49, 53, 130
   history, 48, 49, 51, 53, 55
   and musicians, 49, 54, 55, 58, 59, 60, 61, 62, 63, 64, 67, 75
   reference entry, 126
   reissue in 90s, 112
   vibrato, 49, 58
'67 Reissue, 132
'75 original (fourth version), 89, *91*, 126
'83, 127
'84, 132
'84 original (sixth version), 104, 127
'90, 129
90s reissue of 50s-style, *see* 1958 Korina
'98, 129
400, 129
1958 Korina (reissue), 109, 131
1959 Korina (reissue), 131
Futura model (Corvus-like), 101, 103, 132

'Futura' model (Explorer-like), 16, 17, 25, *27*, 28, 113, 132
Historic Collection, 109, 112
and Ibanez lawsuit, 80
Kalamazoo factory, 9, 10, 89, 97, 101, 118
logs of production data, 19, *22*, 29, 118
Mahogany Futura model, 113, 132
'map' guitar, 103
Marauder model, 89
Moderne model, 16, 17, 18, *30*, 32, 33, 80, 97, 100, *102-103*, 132
Modernistic line, 14, 19, 32, 34, 112
Nashville factory, 89, 97, 101, 108, 118
patent applications, 15, 16, *23*, *27*, *30*
pricelists: 1958, 20, 28, *31*; 1963, 44; 1965, 45; 1966, 49; 1968, 49
RD models, 89, 92, *94-95*, 132
sale of, 101, 104
serial numbers, 133-135
S-1 model, 89
'Thunderbolt' model, *31*, 34, 35
Victory models, 104
Zakk Wylde ZV, 96
zone prices, 20
Gibson Gazette (magazine), 18, 25, *30*, 32
Gibson Mandolin-Guitar Manufacturing, 9
Gibson, Orville, 8, 9
GMW Guitarworks, 96, 99
Gretsch, 13, 35, 41
Grohl, Dave, 113
Gruhn, George / Gruhn Guitars, 57, 69, 76, 109
GTR, *see* Gruhn, George
Guitar Magazine, 33, 34
Guitar Trader, 97

H

Hamer
   Mini V, 67
   and musicians, 61, 67, 71, 73, 75, 79
   Scepter model, 76
   Standard model, 71, 72, 73, *74-75*, 76, *78-79*
   'Thunderbolt' model, 34
   Vector Korina model, 113
   XT model, 73
Hamer, Paul, 69, 72
Hammett, Kirk, 105
Hardtke, Alan, 109

Harris, Norman, 68
Havenga, Clarence, 15, 17, *22*
Haynes, Warren, 113
Hendee, Craig, 69
Hendrix, Jimi, 49, 52, 53, *54*, 112, 114
Hetfield, James, 105, *106*
Holmes, Chris, 114
Huis, John, 10, 14, 56
humbucking pickup, 12, 13

I

Ibanez
   copy guitars, 77, 80, 82
   Destroyer model, 80, 82
   Firebrand model, 80
   Futura model, 80, 82, 100
   and Gibson lawsuit, 80
   history, 77, 80
   Iceman models, 81, *83*
   and musicians, 80, 81, 89
   Rocket Roll models, 80, 82, *82-83*, 91
   Xiphos model, 111
   XV-500 model, *82-83*

J

Jackson
   Double Rhoads Custom model, *94-95*
   King V model, 96
   and musicians, 93, 94, 95, 96, 99, 105, 108, 114
   Randy Rhoads (original) model, *94-95*
   RR (Randy Rhoads) models, 94, 96, 113, 114
   Warrior, *98-99*
Jackson Charvel, *see* Jackson
Jackson, Grover, 57, 58, 92, 93, 94, 95, 96, *98*, 115
Jones, Brian, 48, *51*
Jones, Phil, 108, 109
Jones, Steve, 88
Judas Priest, 61, 67, 73, 75
Juszkiewicz, Henry, 104

K

Kansas, 84, 86
Kaufman, Rob, 61
King, Albert, 45, *46*, 48, 59, 61
King, Kerry, 81, 105
Kinks, The, 8, 48, 50
Kiss, 81, 83

ACKNOWLEDGEMENTS

Andy Powell (September 2010); Michael Schenker (November 2010); Tim Shaw (October 2010); Johnny Winter (December 2010); Dean Zelinsky (October 2010). The sources of any previously published quotations are footnoted where they occur in the text.

THANKS

In addition to those already named in Instrument Pictures, Artist Pictures, Memorabilia, and Original Interviews, the author would like to thank: Julie Bowie, Jayne Andrews, Tony Arambarri (NAMM); Johnny Black, Steve Brown (vintaxe.com), Kev Chilcott (Royale Guitars), Alison B. Curry (Christie's), Paul Day, Luigi Di Dio (Getty Images), Carla Dragotti, Kelly Downes (Selectron), Darren Edwards, Marc Fettarappa, Pat Foley (Gibson), Gil Hembree (*Vintage Guitar Magazine*), Doug Hinman, Christopher Hjort, Dave Hunter, Mike Jefree (*TTJ*), Kerry Keane (Christie's), Alan Korn, Ron Kowalke (*Old Cars Weekly*), Gary Levermore, Brian Majeski (*The Music Trades*), Joel McIver, Ward Meeker (*Vintage Guitar Magazine*), Ron Middlebrook (Centerstream), John Morrish, Régine Moylett, Paul Nelson, Andy Nye, Martina Oliver (Getty Images), Sung-Hee Park (Christie's), John Peden, Greg Prevost, Julian Ridgway (Getty Images), Alan Robinson, Rikky Rooksby, Adam Sagir (Noise Cartel), Chris Scapelliti (*Guitar Aficionado*), Lynn Seager (Divine Recordings), Aron Searle (TRADA), Art Thompson (*Guitar Player*), Jamie Webber, Dale K. Wells (CCCA Museum), Tom Wheeler, Ronald Lynn Wood.

SPECIAL THANKS to Walter Carter for the detailed Reference Listing; to André Duchossoir for sharing documents from his research; and to Martin Kelly for access to his fine paper collection.

BOOKS

Tony Bacon *The History Of The American Guitar* (Balafon/Friedman Fairfax 2001); *The Les Paul Guitar Book* (Backbeat 2009); *Million Dollar Les Paul: In Search Of The Most Valuable Guitar In The World* (Jawbone 2008); *The Stratocaster Guitar Book: A Complete History Of Fender Stratocaster Guitars* (Backbeat 2010).
Tony Bacon (ed) *Echo & Twang* (Backbeat 2001); *Electric Guitars: The Illustrated Encyclopedia* (Thunder Bay 2000), *Fuzz & Feedback* (Backbeat 2000).
Tony Bacon & Paul Day *The Ultimate Guitar Book* (DK/Knopf 1991).
Julius Bellson *The Gibson Story* (Gibson 1973).
Ian C. Bishop *The Gibson Guitar From 1950* (Musical New Services 1977).
Walter Carter *The Gibson Electric Guitar Book: Seventy Years Of Classic Guitars* (Backbeat 2007); *Gibson Guitars: 100 Years Of An American Icon* (GPG 1994).
A.R. Duchossoir *Gibson Electrics – The Classic Years: An Illustrated History Of The Electric Guitars Produced By Gibson Up To The Mid 1960s* (Hal Leonard 1994); *Guitar Identification* (Hal Leonard 1990).
Zachary R. Fjestad & Larry Meiners *Gibson Flying V* (Blue Book 2007).
George Gruhn & Walter Carter *Gruhn's Guide To Vintage Guitars: An Identification Guide For American Fretted Instruments* (Backbeat 2010).
Guitar Trader *Guitar Trader's Vintage Guitar Bulletin Vol. 1 1982* (Bold Strummer 1991); *Guitar Trader's Vintage Guitar Bulletin Vol. 2 1983* (Bold Strummer 1992).
Gil Hembree *Gibson Guitars: Ted McCarty's Golden Era 1948–1966* (G.H. Books 2007).
Dave Hunter *Star Guitars: 101 Guitars That Rocked The World* (Voyageur 2010); *The Electric Guitar Sourcebook: How To Find The Sounds You Like* (Backbeat 2006); *The Guitar Pickups Handbook: The Start Of Your Sound* (Backbeat 2008).
J.T.G. *Gibson Shipping Totals 1946–1979* (J.T.G. 1992).
Bill Rich & Rick Nielsen *Guitars Of The Stars Volume 1 Rick Nielsen* (Gots 1993).
Paul Specht, Michael Wright, Jim Donahue *Ibanez: The Untold Story* (Hoshino 2005).
Tom Wheeler *American Guitars* (HarperPerennial 1990); *The Guitar Book: A Handbook For Electric And Acoustic Guitarists* (MacDonald & Jane's 1975).
Ronald Lynn Wood *Moderne: Holy Grail Of Vintage Guitars* (Centerstream 2008).
We also consulted various back issues of the following magazines: *Beat Instrumental*; *Gibson Gazette*; *Guitar Heroes*; *Guitar Player*; *Guitar Trader's Vintage Guitar Bulletin*; *Guitar World*; *Guitarist*; *Melody Maker*; *The Music Trades*; *Vintage Guitar*.

TRADEMARKS

Throughout this book we have mentioned a number of registered trademark names. Rather than put a trademark or registered symbol next to every occurrence of a trademarked name, we state here that we are using the names only in an editorial fashion and that we do not intend to infringe any trademarks.

UPDATES?

The author and publisher welcome any new information for future editions. Write to: Pointy Guitars, Backbeat/Jawbone, 2A Union Court, 20-22 Union Road, London SW4 6JP, England. Or you can email: pointyguitars@jawbonepress.com

"The pointed end flies in the lead / So when it flies, it's hard to read / You have to be upside-down to see it."
They Might Be Giants 'Flying V' from *Here Come The ABCs* 2005